A NATIONAL PARTY NO MORE

Dedicated to Shirley Carver Miller,
the Mother Lion of our rather large pack
and my companion, critic, and crutch
for fifty years.

A NATIONAL PARTY NO MORE

THE CONSCIENCE OF A CONSERVATIVE DEMOCRAT

ZELL MILLER

STROUD&HALL
PUBLISHERS

Stroud & Hall Publishing
225 Central Avenue
Suite 1608
Atlanta, GA 30303
www.stroudhall.com

The paper used in this publication meets the minimum requirements
of American National Standard for Information Sciences—
Permanence of Paper for Printed Library Materials.
ANSI Z39.48–1984. (alk. paper)

Library of Congress Cataloging-in-Publication Data

Miller, Zell, 1932–
A national party no more: the conscience of a conservative Democrat
by Zell Miller
p. cm.
ISBN 0-9745376-1-6
1. Democratic Party (U.S.)
I. Title.
JK2316.M37 2003
324.2736—dc22

2003019269

Other Books by Zell Miller
The Mountains Within Me (1975), *Great Georgians* (1978),
They Heard Georgia Singing (1980), *Corps Values* (1997)

Zell Miller strikes many notes in this book: nostalgia for his hard-scrabble past in rural Georgia, boundless love for his family and neighbors, pride in his record as one of his state's most popular governors. But at its core is an abiding anger at the tone and direction of the Democratic Party—a party, he believes, that has forfeited its hold on many of those it claims to represent. Miller's political adversaries may reject his premise; they may challenge his evidence; but they will ignore his argument at their peril. Given Miller's extraordinary track record, attention must be paid.

—*Jeff Greenfield*
CNN Senior Analyst

Opposing lower taxes, favoring big government, weak on national defense and homeland security, wrong on capital punishment, abortion, and traditional family values, subservient to interest groups like the AFL-CIO and teachers' unions, lifelong Democrat Georgia Senator Zell Miller makes a powerful election year case that the Democratic party has lost the South and is headed for extinction nationally. A must-read.

—*Lawrence Kudlow*
Co-Host of CNBC's "Kudlow & Cramer"

Had not Zell Miller declared he will never again run for public office, I might get him in serious trouble by calling him "my kind of Democrat." Actually, he is "my kind of American." His memoir is a delightful, good-spirited account of a life of patriotism and public service without malice or mean partisanship. The Democratic Party would be well advised to take his sincere advice, but the certainty that they won't only underlines Senator Miller's concerns about his ancestral party.

—*Robert Novak*
Syndicated Columnist and CNN Political Analyst

For more than forty years, in every position he's held, Zell Miller has exemplified the Marine Corps belief in *Semper Fidelis*. He is a true and proven American patriot who has the courage to tell the truth. This is a book Americans must read because it is a serious work that effectively outlines and defines American politics and culture as they exist today.

—*Newt Gingrich*
Former Speaker, U.S. House of Representatives

Zell Miller's book, *A National Party No More*, is fascinating, provocative, and is a wake-up call for the Democratic Party. Miller blasts interest groups and provides a scathing review of the current Democratic presidential hopefuls.   And, he is unwavering in his support for pro-growth tax rate reductions and tax reform. Miller's candid and sincere assessment of his party and the issues should be taken seriously if Democrats hope for their party to become a governing party once again, as it was from President Roosevelt and Truman to Kennedy and Johnson.

—*Jack Kemp*
Former U.S. Congressman and Vice-Presidential Candidate

This riveting book is a passionate attack on the values and priorities of liberal Democratic politicians by a conservative Democratic Senator from Georgia who has spent a lifetime in local, state, and national politics. It is filled with strong opinions and incisive observations and is a fascinating and unusually frank analysis of Democratic politicians in the modern Senate.

—*Merle Black*
Asa G. Candler Professor of Politics and Government
Emory University

The varied ingredients that make up Zell Miller—mountain man, Marine sergeant, college professor, historian, storyteller, baseball coach, book author, heavy lifter in government at every level from small town mayor to governor of Georgia and the U. S. Senate—make him unique in contemporary American politics, and arguably its purest voice. The Democratic Party, and the country, need to hear and heed. The book also stirs a thought that it's too bad he isn't running for the Big One. Since he isn't, this book is the next best thing. Besides, it's fun to read!

—*Jim Minter*
Former Executive Editor
The Atlanta Journal and Constitution

ACKNOWLEDGMENTS

If you ever see a turtle on a fence post, you know it didn't get there by itself. So it is with getting elected and, yes, with writing a book.

Having a top-notch staff that allows me time to read, think, research, and write is indeed a blessing. I'm a lucky man and I thank them all, including Joan Kirchner, Alex Albert, Frances Wickes, Camille Osborne, John Stacy, and especially the two indispensable aides who have been with me for so long, Toni Brown and Martha Gilland.

Lee Walburn is a longtime friend and the recently retired editor of *Atlanta Magazine*. Although I'm sure he doesn't agree with all this, his taking the time to read my original draft and offer numerous helpful suggestions was a confidence booster and greatly improved the book.

And lastly, having my two yellow Labs, Gus and Woodrow, at my feet as I wrote kept my blood pressure from getting too high.

CONTENTS

FOREWORD
BY CHARLIE COOK

You don't have to be a conservative to see that the Democratic Party has serious problems. In fact, Howard Dean has gone from being an asterisk in the polls to frontrunner as presidential candidate by attacking the direction and leadership of the Democratic Party. While Howard Dean's view of what's wrong with the Democratic Party is obviously different from Zell Miller's view, the fact that prominent Democrats from opposite wings of the party both expound strong condemnations of it tells us a great deal. The Democratic Party lacks direction, vision, and leadership.

In the thirty-one years since I came to Washington in 1972, a college freshman working as an elevator operator in the Senate office buildings, I have seen the number of conservative and moderate Democrats in Congress practically evaporate. The days when you had conservative Democratic senators from the South like Jim Allen and John Sparkman from Alabama, John McClellan from Arkansas, Herman Talmadge and Sam Nunn from Georgia, Allen Ellender and Russell Long from Louisiana, Jim Eastland and John Stennis from Mississippi, and Lloyd Bentsen from Texas were a time when Democrats had little concern about perpetuating their majority in the Senate and, for that matter, in the House as well.

Times changed, and one by one these conservatives retired, died, or in Talmadge's case lost reelection, more often than not replaced by Republicans until eventually, the Democratic majority in the Senate was no more. The Republican tidal wave of 1994 marked a clear demarcation line, when the history of Congress and the national political scene made a clear shift from one period to another, and conservatives in the South became more of a novelty, an exception to the rule rather than the norm. My favorite statistic coming from that election is that not only did Democrats lose their majority of the Congressional seats from Georgia, Senator Zell Miller's home state, but within six months of that election, there were more retired Republican dentists (three) in the Georgia U.S. House delegation than there were white Democrats (one). In small-town and rural America and across the South and the border South, Democrats have problems.

Senator Zell Miller's new book, *A National Party No More*, is part memoir, part debate case, part spleen venting, but all compelling reading. It is a journal from his odyssey growing up in the mountains to the Georgia Governor's Mansion and the U.S. Senate. But it is also about the lessons and observations he has gathered over the course of a fascinating career in politics that Democrats would be well advised to read and chew over.

This is certainly not to say that all is perfect in the Republican Party; indeed, just as Democrats are having horrible difficulties in rural areas, in small towns, and in the South, Republicans are encountering their own problems among suburban voters outside of the South, with many of the same social and cultural issues that are driving white voters away from the Democratic Party in the South driving suburban voters, particularly women, away from the Republican Party in the rest of the country. But it is because the South was so monolithically Democratic before and is now, outside of its larger cities, becoming so Republican that these problems Democrats have are more acute those facing the GOP.

Someone else can write a book about the challenges facing the Republican Party. Zell Miller has taken on the problems of the Democratic Party and articulated them with clarity and candor, but also with humor and regret. It's clear that the problems Miller sees in his party are problems that hurt him. A sense of anguish and honesty takes the edge off and keeps the book from coming across as a tirade or a way to settle scores.

With any luck, this book will set off a spirited debate over the future of the Democratic Party that is badly needed and long overdue.

Charlie Cook

Editor and Publisher, *Cook Political Report*

Political Analyst, *National Journal* and NBC News

INTRODUCTION

BY GRIFFIN B. BELL

United States Senator Zell Miller is perhaps the most experienced public official in our nation. He has served in the state government of Georgia as an administrator of a number of vital agencies, as an assistant to two governors, as head of the State Democratic Party, as Lieutenant Governor, and then as Governor.

His father died when he was only a few weeks old and he was raised by his mother in a single parent home. He served in the U.S. Marine Corps and has taught at four different colleges. His background is such that he understands people and their hopes and aspirations.

Zell not only believes in our constitutional system but understands it. He knows that in order to govern, the views of everyone must be accommodated to the greatest extent possible. He knows that there is no room for special interest groups to get more than their share. In short, his idea of representative government is that there is a common good and that each of us owes allegiance to the common good.

Upon entering the Senate, Zell Miller made his position very clear to the people of Georgia. He stated that he was not representing the Democrats or the Republicans, but that he would represent all of the people of Georgia. He has been faithful to that promise. But in the meantime, it is becoming clear that Senator Miller is right: the Democratic Party is no longer a national party in the sense of seeking to represent the common good as it may be implicated in national questions involving all sections of our country.

Only time will tell whether the Democratic Party will wither on the vine, as happened to the Whig Party over the issue of slavery. The Whigs were a strong party that disintegrated over a period of about ten years after the Compromise of 1850 with part going to the Republican Party and part to the Democratic Party. A national party must deserve to exist if it is to exist.

President Franklin Roosevelt, the greatest Democratic president of our time, knew this when he said that the Democratic Party was a big tent with room for all. That presupposed that those in the tent would be dedicated to the common good rather than to the good of each special interest group.

Senator Richard Russell once observed that politics is the art of compromise. That concept has been replaced by the guerrilla warfare being fought with the weapon of the sixty-vote filibuster rule, where nothing can be done in the Senate unless there are sixty potential votes. Judicial nominees are blocked even when there is a majority in favor of advising and consent to the nomination by the president. A majority of the Senate is no longer sufficient.

Hopefully, Senator Miller's fine book will help end the partisan warfare and restore democracy and common sense in the Senate. The American people cannot and will not be governed by a minority in the Senate much longer.

Griffin B. Bell
Appointed by President John F. Kennedy
as U.S. Circuit Judge, 1961-1976
Appointed by President Jimmy Carter
as the 72nd Attorney General of the United States, 1977-1979

A CONSCIENCE SHAPED

1

There will be those who ask, "What is this all about, *The Conscience of a Conservative Democrat?*" I can hear the liberal Washington crowd right now. Gold medalists in the Sneering Olympics, hissing, "In the first place, Miller's no Democrat." On the other hand, there are some die-hard Republicans back in Georgia who will break out their choicest cuss words and swear, "He's no conservative." And you can bet that some old drinking buddies from many years ago will slap their knees and hoot, "What conscience?"

I once heard an old mountaineer say on the matter of giving opinions, "I'm not a judge and there ain't enough of me to be a jury." Nevertheless, in this short treatise I've put down some strong opinions. It's not important to me that you agree with everything I say. But it's important to me that I get it said. This is about things that matter most to me, what I believe in today, and, most of all, why I've come to believe these things.

I have arrived at a station in life where I hear the whistle of that moral policeman we all have to answer to when it comes to living a life . . . or serving in office. So at this point I'm more interested in pleasing the sternest critic of all than I am in appeasing those who might question my loyalty to the Democratic Party, those who question my conservative credentials, or those who say I simply put a finger to the wind and zigzag in whatever way it happens to be blowing. I'm of the same mind as John F. Kennedy, who wrote in *Profiles in Courage* that "when party and office holder differ as to how the national interest is to be served, we must place the first responsibility we owe not to our party or even to our constituents, but to our individual consciences."

Sigmund Freud wrote that the human psyche is divided into three components: the id, the ego, and the superego. The latter is best known as "conscience." Freud believed a balance of all three was necessary to keep a person from going off the deep end. Now, I admit I don't know much about all this Freudian stuff. After all, he was a psychiatrist, and I've never known one of those who didn't need one himself.

What I do know, however, is that my conscience travels with me everywhere I go, like some unwelcome inner companion. I cannot escape him and is he tough. He is on steroids, has a Black Belt and long fingernails, and stomps around inside of me, sometimes in hobnailed boots. He's been there as long as I can remember. Although it's getting tougher and tougher for me to blow out all the candles on my birthday cake, he just grows stronger . . . and louder. A long time ago I would try to anesthetize him with alcohol, but since the beatings grew worse when he sobered up, I decided to quit buying him drinks.

These days I've come to better understand why my conscience is the way it is. When I think of the many different jobs I've had, not to mention all the saints and sinners and sots I've known along the way, I realize that those broad and sometimes harsh experiences have made me who I am. This is also why I can't stand the thought of meeting my Maker without advising members of my Democratic Party and other politicians who are so far out of touch with regular Americans to "shape up."

If Thomas Jefferson and Andrew Jackson lived today, they would have a great lawsuit against the Democratic Party for consumer fraud. What the party stands for in no way resembles what those great leaders believed about governing, especially Jefferson, who didn't even like political parties. He also strongly opposed taxes and wanted a government limited in size and scope. He would be appalled by the powerful hodgepodge of special interest groups that actually run the party he created, the party that now opposes tax cuts and strives for more and bigger government. The Sage of Virginia dreamed of a nation of small stakeholders and citizen lawmakers, not special interest groups that want to elect their pet incumbents over and over.

The national party is so far adrift we shouldn't even call our annual fund-raisers Jefferson-Jackson dinners. In the eyes of Middle America, it has become a value-neutral party. Everyone knows the key issues: capital punishment, late-term abortion (even with a lot of pro-choice people), trying violent juveniles as adults, national defense, and the teaching of values in school (though not necessarily prayer.) As issues, these trump prescription drug costs and health care, as important as those two issues are and as much as we need to address them. John J. Zogby, the prominent pollster, once put it this way: "We live in a new world, but with old values."

Too many in my party do not understand this. But I wonder how many would understand if they had had experiences similar to mine?

In 1944, when I was a thin twelve-year-old, I stood on busy Peachtree Street in Atlanta, weighted down in a big, heavy, plastic "Mr. Peanut" costume that began two feet above my head and went down to my knees. My job was to spoon roasted Planter's Peanuts from a bowl to passersby. Four years later, for three dollars a day, I worked on a timber cutting crew at a mountain sawmill. I have been a sergeant in the U.S. Marines, a mobile home salesman, a dishwasher, a bartender, a short order cook, and a college baseball coach. I've been a middle school truant and a college dropout, and I've been a history professor in four different colleges and universities. I've worked for three very different Georgia governors. I've labored in all areas of the criminal justice system—probation, corrections, and parole. I've spoken to less than a dozen people from the back of a pickup truck in the piney woods of South Georgia, and I've spoken to millions by way of national television from Madison Square Garden in New York City. I've been mayor of a town of 300 and the governor of the tenth largest state in the nation. I've written and published books, songs, and poems. I've been the chairman of the board of a very small rural bank, and I've been the chairman of the board of an international real estate development company. I've spent the night in a filthy jail cell, and I've spent the night in the Lincoln Bedroom. I lived for years in a house made out of rocks my mother gathered from a nearby creek, with only an open fireplace for heat, no electricity, no indoor plumbing, no car, no phone, and no father; I've also lived in a 24,000-square-foot Greek Revival mansion with a dozen bathrooms and been chauffeured around by state troopers and my own team of private pilots, with a fleet of planes and helicopters at my beck and call.

I could go on with these contrasts, but suffice it to say that I've lived a long time, and I've seen squalor and I've seen elegance. I've been to the mountaintop and I've been down in the swamp. I've seen bright lights and the darkness of midnight and all the dull shades of gray in between. All of them, for better or for worse, for richer or for poorer, in sickness and in health, have combined to make me what I am.

Whatever I am, whoever I am, wherever I have been, whatever I have done, I couldn't have survived without Shirley Miller. For almost half a century, I have been blessed with a smart and strong wife, a dean's list college student who was on her way to becoming a lawyer. She gave up her dream to go live with a Marine private in an 8-x-24-foot decaying trailer in the Camp Geiger trailer park at Camp LeJune, North Carolina. Later, with one baby in diapers and another on the way, she rode shotgun as we pulled a small U-Haul

With Shirley in Washington.

loaded with all our worldly possessions to Athens, Georgia, where I, not she, would get a college education.

Her entire life has been a sacrifice bunt with me on base. In case you're not into baseball, that means the batter gives himself up and makes an out on purpose so that the runner can advance and hopefully score. To dwell on this today causes pangs of conscience beyond expression. Later on, I will tell you more about Shirley, because if her quiet mountain wisdom had not come to my rescue a few years ago, I wouldn't have had the honor of serving my country as senator from Georgia.

Mountain logic, small-town pragmatism—that's what I've always fallen back on when I didn't know which way to go. In his Pulitzer Prize-winning book, *The Americans: The Democratic Experience*, Daniel Boorstein writes that life is "more graspable" in smaller places. One could find few smaller places than Young Harris, Georgia, in which "to grasp." From the day I was born in

1932 until today, this town's population has hovered around three hundred residents with about four hundred college students.

In 1885, a Methodist circuit rider started a school for seven mountain children in this beautiful but isolated mountain place called Brasstown Valley. It grew into an academy and college named for Judge Young Harris, its chief benefactor, who wanted to help the underprivileged young people who lived in that mountain area. Like honeysuckle in an old fence, this educational institution and my life are inextricably interwoven. I was born and reared in its shadow. Both my parents taught in its classrooms, as did I. Shirley and I were students there.

In 1999, after many, many years in the political arena, I went back to Young Harris to live in the old home place and teach again at this little college that had nurtured me as a shy mountain youth. It was glorious being back in Brasstown Valley with our huge family nearby and as much time as I liked to run my yellow Labs, Gus and Woodrow, across the ridges and along the creeks I had known as a child. It was an idyllic existence.

Then on July 20, 2000, Georgia's senior U.S. Senator Paul Coverdell suddenly died. He had been a good friend and an excellent public servant. We had worked closely together for years, even though he was a Republican and I a Democrat.

A couple of days after the funeral, then-Governor Roy Barnes came to see me in Young Harris. He said he wanted to appoint me to the seat and that I would have to run a few months later in the November general election. I told him I didn't really want to do it, that we were happy being back home. He urged me to think about it, and as he went out the door, he turned and announced solemnly, "I don't have a plan B."

Shirley and I did not sleep much that night. As a younger man, I had very much wanted to go to Washington. I had run unsuccessfully for Congress in 1964 and 1966 and even challenged Herman Talmadge in 1980 for his Senate seat. After a bloody primary and runoff, Republican Mack Mattingly defeated Talmadge in the general election.

Now we were older and wiser, making money, and as happy as we had ever been. But what an opportunity! The chance of a lifetime to be a member of "the nation's most exclusive club" and "world's greatest deliberative body." So we tossed and turned and next morning stared at each other over our oatmeal. How do you say no to the governor?

Finally, Shirley spat it out, "It's what you do, isn't it?"

As usual she hit the mark. Politics was what we had done practically all of our lives. This could be the sixth decade in public life for me. If elected, I would join Richard Russell and Herman Talmadge as one of only three Georgians to be elected both governor and senator.

"Will you go back and forth to Washington with me?" I asked.
"Of course."

"I'm not going to do this partisan stuff," I said.
"I know," she replied.

She repeated my old mantra: "It's not whose team you're on, it's whose side you're on." I picked up the phone and called Georgia's governor.

Governor Barnes made the announcement a few days later in his office. I thanked him. I promised I would be a candidate in November. Then I looked out at a press corps that had covered me for many years and knew me well. I measured my words carefully, knowing after all these years that it was through them I could speak to the people of the state that has been so good to me.

When I left the governor's office and returned to Young Harris to work and to teach, the fires of political ambition that had burned so long and so strong within me had finally cooled. And these last two years with Shirley and our family have been the happiest of my life. And then tragedy struck, and duty called.

Despite the very real reluctance I feel about leaving that old rock house my mother built, I have an obligation to give but one response when my governor asks me to serve, the same response that was drilled into me at boot camp in Parris Island: "Yes, sir."

Governor, I pledge to you that I will serve no single party, but rather seven-and-a-half million Georgians. And every day I serve I will do my best to do so in the same spirit of dignity, integrity, and bipartisan cooperation that were the hallmarks of Paul Coverdell's career.

It is my honor—and my duty—to serve Georgia once again.

And so, Mr. Miller went to Washington. I wish I could say the experience has been like Jimmy Stewart's in *Mr. Smith Goes to Washington.* I wish I could say that I found Washington all I had ever dreamed it to be, the place where the great issues of the day are debated and solved, and great giants walk those hallowed halls. I so wanted Robert Louis Stevenson to be wrong when he wrote, "It is better to travel hopefully than to arrive."

Unfortunately, what I discovered in Washington was truth, and truth did not set me free. It simply made me mad. It filled me with anger on behalf of Americans. You might still ask why I would want to take my own party to the woodshed. The answer is simple: my conscience made me do it.

A NATIONAL PARTY NO MORE

Once upon a time, the most successful Democratic leader of them all, FDR, looked south and said, "I see one-third of a nation ill-housed, ill-clad, ill-nourished." Today our national Democratic leaders look south and say, "I see one-third of a nation and it can go to hell."

Too harsh? I don't think so. Consider these facts. In 1960, the state of Georgia gave the Democratic nominee John F. Kennedy a higher percentage of its vote than JFK's home state of Massachusetts. "You can look it up," as Casey Stengel used to say. Only the percentage in Rhode Island was greater. And Georgians were not disappointed in Kennedy's performance as a chief executive. He stared down the Russians over Cuba and he cut taxes in a significant way that stimulated the economy. Had he not been assassinated, he could have carried Georgia a second time.

In the last nine elections, except for 1976 when regional pride was a huge factor and native son Jimmy Carter lost only Virginia among the eleven states of the old Confederacy, the scoreboard read like this: In 1968 Hubert Humphrey carried Texas because of

Lyndon Johnson, but no other state. Jimmy Carter in 1980 carried only Georgia; the others left the incumbent. In 1992, another native son of the South, Bill Clinton, carried these four: Georgia, Arkansas, Louisiana, and Tennessee. In 1996, Clinton carried Arkansas, Louisiana, Tennessee, and Florida. So, four times—1972, 1984, 1988, and 2000—the Democratic candidate couldn't carry a single Southern state. Not one! Zero! Zilch! And two times, 1968 and 1980, only one Southern state favored the Democratic candidate.

Either the party is not a national party or the candidates were not national candidates. Take your pick. But there is more to this sorry tale. Most recently, in the mid-term elections of 2002, not a single national leader could come to the South to campaign without doing more harm than good. They were strangers in a foreign land. No, not exactly strangers—they were too well-known. That was the problem.

National Chairman Terry McAuliffe couldn't come. He was too liberal. Former President Bill Clinton couldn't come. He was too liberal. The party's titular head, Al Gore of Tennessee, who two years earlier had put up a big fat zero in the region, couldn't come. He was too liberal. Senate Majority Leader Tom Daschle couldn't come. He was too liberal. Unfortunately, he did send his own personal albatross of partisan wrangling on homeland security just weeks before the election for Senator Max Cleland to wear around his neck like the ancient mariner in the Coleridge poem. House Minority Leader Dick Gephardt couldn't come. He was too liberal. Little has changed, except that Nancy Pelosi has taken the place of Gephardt, which makes it even worse. In 2004, none of the leadership can come. When it comes to romancing the South, they bring their flowery bouquets wrapped in old, dried-up carpetbag containers.

So, if this is a national party, sushi is our national dish. If this is a national party, surfboarding has become our national pastime. These people leading our party and those asking to lead our country are like a bunch of naive fraternity boys who don't know what they don't know.

Albert Einstein reportedly once said that someone who keeps doing the same thing over and over, thinking they will get a different result, is insane. Einstein said it, I didn't. But it sure applies to the Democratic Party of recent vintage.

The latest fad—and another way to spend money—is for candidates for the presidency to hire a consultant that specializes in how to campaign in the South or with rural voters. That takes the prize, but I'm open-minded. Please tell me just how one learns how to campaign in the South. Are they instructed to read old Lewis Grizzard books like *Chili Dogs Only Bark at Night* or Jeff Foxworthy's *You Might Be a Redneck If...*? Maybe they convene a focus group on the accents of the candidates. Or a kind of debate prep with questions like, which is the larger NASCAR track, Talladega or Bristol? Or, what is George Jones's nickname, and can you name three of his hit songs? Or, what is a trout line? What is the difference between a violin and a fiddle? Why can't mules reproduce? Perhaps, instead of a debate, they could hold a contest on who could run a chainsaw the best or who could back a pickup with a bass boat or horse trailer attached. This has to be the silliest thing to come along since political consulting became the costly and ridiculous racket it is.

The biggest problem with the party leadership is that they know nothing about the modern South. They still see it as a land of magnolias and mint juleps, with the pointy-headed KKK lurking in the background, waiting to burn a cross or lynch blacks and Jews.

They are like Shreve McCannon, the Canadian in William Faulkner's *Absalom, Absalom!*, who asks the Southerner Quentin Compson, "Tell me about the South. What's it like there? What do they do there? Why do they live there? Why do they live at all?" The modern South and rural America are as foreign to our Democratic leaders as some place in Asia or Africa. In fact, they are more so. At least the leaders go to those other foreign lands to learn about "information-seeking CODEL" (congressional delegation) trips. I'm sure each one could explain the culture and economy of Pakistan, Taiwan, or Kenya better than that of the American South.

Truth is, average Americans, especially those who follow the job market, know a lot more about the South than does the leadership of our party. They know the South has become a land of great promise with an unlimited future. It isn't rusting and rotting away like a lot of places up North. Recent census statistics listing the 100 fastest growing counties in the country showed two-thirds are in the South. Many of them are immigrants from the Blue states.

Today, if you were to separate fifteen Southeastern states from the rest of the Union (I'm not advocating that; eleven tried once), their economy alone would rank as the third largest in the world behind only the United States as a whole and Japan. Its population would be far greater than New England. Georgia alone has the seventeenth-largest economy in the world, larger than Singapore, Hong Kong, or Saudi Arabia. This region is not the backwoods our party leadership seems to think it is. So, think again.

Fiber-optic cable was developed in the South. Atlanta not only has three times more fiber-optic lines than New York City, it is located at the most significant fiber-optic intersection in North America. It is also the region where the modem and the IRMA board were developed, where the first mobile satellite uplink was produced. Georgia was the first state to deliver insurance-reimbursable medical care by telecommunication. The *New York Times* even called it "sophisticated." I was so shocked by the *Times* calling anything down South sophisticated, I cut out the article and saved it.

Nearly a third of the Fortune 500 companies have headquarters located in the region. In Georgia, Porsche moved its headquarters from Nevada, UPS from Connecticut, and Georgia-Pacific from Washington. CNN, Home Depot, Delta, Coca-Cola, and many others started here. This region the national Democrats find so hard to understand and campaign in is further along in racial politics than they could ever imagine—or choose to believe. Minority

Southerners now complete high school at the same rate as white students and the percentage of minority Southerners with college degrees tripled in the past twenty-five years. Recently, when *Newsweek* named "the cream of the crop" of high schools, seven of the top ten were in the South, as were twenty-two of the top fifty. Consider this: in 1990 there were 565 African-Americans holding elective office in the eleven states of the Old Confederacy. You know what the number was in 2000? Almost ten times that number: 5,579. In Georgia, seven African-Americans have been elected statewide in a state that is 70 percent white. Three of those have been elected twice.

While Senator Max Cleland and Governor Roy Barnes were losing with about 46 to 47 percent of the vote in 2002, two African-Americans, Attorney General Thurbert Baker and Commissioner of Labor Michael Thurmond, were getting 56 to 57 percent. In the process they were carrying predominately white counties over-whelmingly, as they had four years before.

I could continue citing additional facts like these for pages. As Dizzy Dean once said, "If you've done it, it ain't bragging." As governor, I used to spend a lot of time selling our region overseas. Other Southern governors did as well. South Carolina's Carroll Campbell was the best of all. In the early 1970s, Jimmy Carter was the first governor to put a Georgia office overseas, one in Brussels and one in Tokyo. In the 1990s we expanded that to nine and there were 1,600 foreign businesses in our state. Of course, this may not compare to places like New York and California, but the point I'm making is that this is not the South our Democratic Party leaders think it is. The South they have stuck in their minds is gone with the wind.

After being involved in or observing elections for more than forty years, I've learned a few things about Democrats in Washington. They always act as if the last election never happened. They also believe in purity. Do they ever?! Like that old Ivory Soap commercial, 99.44/100 percent pure is all that will do. You cannot agree on just seven of their ten issues, or even nine. All ten must be embraced and ostentatiously hugged to your bosom with slobbering kisses. Remember how Democrats wouldn't let Governor Bob Casey of Pennsylvania even speak at our national conventions because he was pro-life? That was keeping the convention "pure."

National Democratic leaders are as nervous as a long-tailed cat around a rocking chair when they travel south or get out in rural America. They have no idea what to say or how to act. I once saw one try to eat a boiled shrimp without peeling it. Talk about crunchy. Another one loudly gagged on the salty taste of country ham.

Democrats have never seen a snail darter they didn't want to protect, but sometimes I think the one endangered species they don't want to save is the Southern conservative Democrat. However, they do want to use us ever so often, usually in the fall every other year. We're like that alcoholic uncle families try to hide in a room up in the attic. But, after the primaries are over and the general election nears, Democrats trot out the South and show us off—at arm's length, of course—as if to say "Look how tolerant we are; see how caring? Why, we even allow people "like this" in our party of the big tent. We still love that strange old reprobate uncle. He's still a member of our big family." Then, as soon as the election is over the old boy is banished to the attic, ignored for another two years when we go get him and crowd him up under the party tent that now has shrunk to the size of a dunce cap.

Al Gore became only the third Democrat since the Civil War to lose every state in the Old Confederacy, plus two border states as well. George McGovern and Walter Mondale were the others. But they had an excuse: they were crushed in national landslides. They didn't just lose the South. They lost from sea to shining sea. Gore's loss was different. Had he won any state in the Old Confederacy or one more border state, he would be president today. But it didn't happen. Gore lost his home state of Tennessee, Bill Clinton's home state of Arkansas, and the Democratic bastion of West Virginia.

Even Michael Dukakis—hardly a son of the South—didn't manage to lose there.

The campaign in the South was a mess, and it didn't have to happen. There were more Democratic than Republican governors in the region, and the Democrats held a majority of state legislative chambers. Largely because of the Democratic debacle in the South in 2002, even that has changed; three Democratic governors also bit the dust.

Chances are it's going to happen again. Given the demographic changes that determine the makeup of the House of Representatives and the Electoral College, it will be worse. In 2004, if we have the exact same popular-vote split between the Democratic and Republican candidates, and if these candidates win the same states, the Electoral College margin for the Republican will get bigger. How much bigger? The Republican candidate would have a majority in the Electoral College not by four electors, as George W. Bush did in 2000, but by eighteen.

Obviously, Southerners believe the national Democratic Party does not share their values. They do not trust the national party with their money or the security of the country.

If Southern voters think you don't understand them—or even worse, much worse, if they think you look down on them—they will never vote for you. Folks in the South have a simple way of saying this: "He's not one of us." When a politician hears those words, he's already dead.

The point I'm making is that for Southern voters, the issues you choose to talk about—or not talk about—are as important as the positions you take on those issues. Southern voters may say they're for gun control, and they may well be for gun control, but they simply don't trust anybody who spends too much time talking about it. Bill Clinton understood that. Al Gore did not.

As I said, the most important values for Southerners are related to the questions of money and trust. Recently, our party leaders seemed to think that the choice was between cutting taxes and controlling spending on the one side and enacting the Democratic agenda on the other. I disagreed. Long experience in government has taught me that if you don't look and act as if you are serious with the people's money, they won't trust you with any more of it. Why should they?

There was a time—and it wasn't long ago—when the leaders of my party understood both the policy and political value of cutting taxes. The Kennedy-Johnson tax bill in 1964 cut all tax brackets, including at the top. It was passed by an overwhelmingly Democratic Congress as part of an aggressive agenda that, within a year, included the creation of Medicare—the most significant health-care initiative in American history.

And how did opponents attack the Kennedy-Johnson proposal? As fiscally irresponsible, because it didn't pay off the debt and was nothing more than a quick fix. Who was attacking these tax cuts back then? Why, lo and behold, it was Republicans! It was a political fiasco for them. The Republicans would not gain control of either the House or the Senate for a generation, and not until they had reversed their party's position on cutting taxes.

I know from personal experience that you can be a Democrat and have a solid Democratic agenda while cutting taxes and holding the line on spending. When I was governor of Georgia, we cut taxes by almost a billion dollars, reduced spending, and cut personnel by 5,000 positions.

That was why I was able to raise the salaries of university professors and public school teachers to the highest in the South and get a lottery passed by the voters in my Bible Belt state. Then we provided pre-kindergarten education for every four-year-old in the state; technical training for every high school graduate; and the HOPE Scholarship, which gives every Georgia student who has a B average, and maintains it, a tuition-free college education—every one!

But if the people in my state hadn't trusted the government with their money—if we hadn't simultaneously cut taxes and controlled spending—these progressive education measures would have been taken apart, labeled as "big spending" by a Democratic governor.

We Democrats can have an aggressive agenda for America. But we need to remember that talking about an agenda is quite different from getting it done. For us to get it done, the people we serve have to trust us. And right now not enough of them do, especially in the South.

There is always a lesson to be learned from studying the British. Remember how the Conservative Party with towering figures like Margaret Thatcher dominated that country's politics for eighteen years until the Labor Party led by Tony Blair was able to reclaim power? It happened because Blair took his party kicking and screaming toward the middle of the political spectrum. The extreme left wing of the party was obliterated and the influence of the trade union was greatly diminished, but not completely destroyed. If Clinton had followed through and governed as he had campaigned, it would have happened here for the Democrats.

For many years now in the South, the magic formula for the Democratic nominee to win in a general election against a Republican is to get 40 percent of the white vote and 90 percent of the African-American vote. Increasingly over the years it has been easier to get 90 percent of the African-American vote than 40 percent of the white vote. I believe that the margin of African-American votes for the Democrats is going to change soon. It only has to change a fraction in the South to make a huge difference. Ralph Reed, the brilliant strategist and former Republican state chairman of Georgia understands this, as does Bush strategist Karl Rove and many other Republicans.

It will be similar to what happened in a couple of governor's races in Virginia in the 1990s. Virginia Republicans figured out some time ago that they were not going to get many more white votes, so what did they do? They started quietly going after African-American support. First, George Allen and then later James Gilmore each received nearly 20 percent of the African-American vote in their races for governor, just by reaching out and really working for it. Going after this constituency required no compromise of other issues and it accomplished two things in Virginia. It directly cost the Democrats core votes and, by moderating the look of the Republican Party, it indirectly cost the Democrats swing votes. Using this strategy, Allen and Gilmore crushed their Democratic opponents in successful elections in 1993 and 1997. To his credit, Democrat Mark Warner made sure that didn't happen to him in 2001.

There are a growing and increasingly wealthy number of African-American professionals and managers in Georgia. And they will not be led by the once powerful civil rights leaders of the past. A good example is Herman Cain, the former president and CEO of the Godfather's Pizza chain, an African-American presently running for the United States Senate seat in Georgia as a Republican. He's not the only one. Al Bartell is also in this race that includes two traditional white Republican congressmen.

Time will only tell the effect of seeing President George W. Bush surround himself with African-Americans like Secretary of State Colin Powell, National Security Advisor Condoleezza Rice, and Deputy Attorney General Larry Thompson. But one thing is for sure, the automatic 90 percent for Democrats in the South will sooner rather than later be just a memory.

It will be difficult for the Democratic Party to nominate a candidate capable of winning nationwide until it abandons the suicidal compulsion of allowing Iowa and New Hampshire to be the tail that always wags the Democratic donkey. Don't misunderstand me. These are good states with good people living in them and good people representing them in public offices. But, not by any stretch of one's imagination can the Iowa Democratic caucus be interpreted as representative of the nation. More to the truth, it is simply allowing labor unions to make this most important first decision. And those first decisions more often than not become the ultimate decision.

Consider this: there are 32,000 unionized teachers and 28,000 members of AFSCME in Iowa—and are they activists! In 2000, with a hot contest between Al Gore and Bill Bradley, the Iowa caucuses drew 61,000 participants. Add up the above numbers and guess who were the ones who turned out. By the way, there are four counties in Georgia alone that vote more than twice that number. New Hampshire is a great state, but a microcosm of America it is not. Isn't it strange that based on the outcome in these two states a Democratic candidate will be chosen? No, it's more than strange; it's suicide.

While I have dwelled primarily on the problems of the Democratic Party in the South and rural America, their problem is much greater than that. The national Democratic Party is in eminent danger of being cannibalized, eaten alive by the special interest groups with their single-issue constituents who care about only their own narrow agenda. This is exactly what happened to the Whig Party as the Civil War loomed on the horizon. With self-interest rampant among a lot of different groups, the center would not hold and the party died.

I own a fiddle that supposedly belonged to Zeb Vance, the great North Carolina mountaineer who was elected governor in 1862. He opposed much of what Confederate President Jefferson Davis was doing in Richmond. He was too young to be involved in the Whig Party at the height of its popularity, but he had been "born a Whig" and many thought this moderate, independent-minded, vigorous young leader might be the one to keep the party alive in the South. When he was approached to do so in 1865, Vance was typically direct: "The party is dead and buried and the tombstone placed over it and I don't care to spend the rest of my days mourning at its grave."

Like that Whig Party of the late 1850s, the Democratic Party of today has become dangerously fragmented, and considering the present leadership it can only get worse. "All the king's horses and all the king's men" can't put this party back together again.

Compromise will become increasingly difficult and no leader's goal will be to reach consensus or common ground. Instead, they will more than ever blindly champion this group and that group.

The special interest groups have come between the Democratic Party and the people. The Party is no longer a link to most Americans. Each advocacy group has become more important than the sum of the whole. It is a rational party no more. It is a national party no more. So, bang the drum slowly and play the fife lowly, for the sun is setting over a waiting grave.

BORN A DEMOCRAT—
MARRIED A DEMOCRAT

3

I was born a Democrat. It's not simply a party affiliation; it's more like a birthmark for me and many of my fellow mountaineers. There's actually a small pinkish spot on the back of my neck just like my father's. Both the birthmark and allegiance to the Democratic Party have been handed down in my family from one generation to the next. Time does not erase it. It is part of our DNA.

I would no more think of changing parties than I would think of changing my name. To change would be like walking on my mother's grave. Her maiden name was Birdie Bryan, and she took pride that we may have been related to the old Democratic warhorse, William Jennings Bryan. It doesn't matter that we're not. Political heritage was important in the Appalachian Mountains where Georgia, North and South Carolina, and Tennessee come together.

Politics there wasn't simply a political-year pastime. It was extremely serious business that divided neighbors and caused feuds. Sometimes, lives were lost because of it. Politics in this neck of the woods wasn't for the faint-hearted. It was rough—some might say strange—and I cut my political teeth in this area, in this atmosphere.

In those days, Democrats bought gasoline only at service stations owned by Democrats, and Republicans shopped only at stores owned by Republicans. Parents in Democratic families frowned on their offspring marrying or even dating Republicans and vice versa. Last names immediately told one the party to which a person belonged. All Taylors, Brysons, Dentons, Carvers, Plotts, and Millers were Democrats; all the Corns, Wests, Shooks, Woods, and Berrys were Republicans.

This area had been Indian Territory until gold was discovered in North Georgia in 1828, twenty years before the rush to California. The gold lured explorers and prospectors into the foothills of Nacoochee Valley and nearby Dahlonega. But only the hardiest and most courageous settlers pushed over Unicoi and Tesnatee Gaps into the higher, rugged mountain country to the north that was being vacated by the Indians.

My great-great-grandfather on my father's side was one of the pioneers, arriving in 1835 as a new county was being formed. When asked what the Legislature should name this new county, someone replied, "Union, for none but Union men reside in it."

Significantly, there is also a Union County in the mountains of Tennessee, South Carolina, and North Carolina. One reason is that in those places and at that time, slavery was not the controversial issue. President Andrew Jackson, their neighbor from Tennessee, was a man these frontiersmen admired. He had removed the Indians and drawn the line between sectional interests and Union loyalty. "Old Hickory" had said in a famous toast, "To our Union, it must be preserved." His vice president, John C. Calhoun of South Carolina, answered, "To our Union, after our liberties most dear," and then resigned his office.

That same kind of division exerted itself in 1861 when these mountain counties opposed secession, which by then revolved around the issue of slavery. Like most frontiersmen, mountaineers were self-sufficient. They were not slave owners.

Mountaineers had little in common with the large plantation owners of the Piedmont and Coastal Plains who raised cotton and owned slaves. Most of the legislators representing mountain counties in four states voted against secession. But despite significant anti-secessionist and anti-Civil War sentiment, even families became divided to the point where it was commonplace for one brother to serve in the Confederate army and another in the Union army. Vengeance Creek, which flows not far from my home, was so named because of a family whose members not only fought on opposing sides, but even killed one another over the war issue.

That kind of political separation continued in volatile but, thankfully, less violent ways. When I was growing up, virtually all of our neighbors were Republicans. They were wonderful neighbors who would give us the shirts off their backs. They shared sausage and ham when they killed a hog and were the first to help when one of us was sick or in need. We loved and respected them and they loved and respected us. But they would not vote for me or anyone else who was a Democrat.

My mother, Birdie Bryan Miller, was a Democrat through and through and wouldn't have altered her devotion even in appreciation of the help from those kind neighbors. Obviously, she had a lasting influence on me. She was the most determined person I've ever known, a characteristic that perhaps rubbed off on me to the extent some might even refer to me as stubborn. She was born in 1893 on a South Carolina farm and was just a child when her mother died. Her father married again relatively soon, and half brothers and sisters soon added to the growing Bryan clan.

Her memories of her childhood in this large family were pleasant. She was the tomboy of the family. She could run faster and work harder than any others, yet at the same time she had this thing about painting pictures. Her talent was obvious and her father urged her to pursue it. When she finished college he sent her to New

York City to study at the prestigious Art Students League. The Empire City was worldly to a young woman reared in the rural South. But she learned not to blush when she sketched nude women—or even men wearing skimpy loincloths.

Like thousands of artists before and after, Birdie Bryan soon discovered no great demand for her talents. Jobs for artists were scarce everywhere and nonexistent in Leesville, South Carolina. Fortunately, she came across an ad in an educational bulletin that announced the need for an art teacher at a mountain college named Young Harris over in Georgia.

She responded and was accepted. Early in fall 1919, her train, which was running an hour late, pulled into the railroad depot at Murphy, North Carolina. It was already three o'clock in the afternoon, and when she hauled her baggage from the train, a three-seater stagecoach drawn by two big black mules awaited her.

The seats were already filled with students, and the driver seemed a little miffed about having to wait. He started the mules in a gallop. The road from Murphy to Young Harris, then as now, curves along the high bluffs above the Hiawassee River. My mother remembered fearing that the "hack," as it was called, would plunge any minute to the rocky river below. The trip from Murphy to Young Harris by stagecoach took six hours. The stagecoach pulled onto the dark, silent college campus at nine o'clock.

The tired new art teacher was fed and given a room in the girls' dormitory. The next morning, when she looked around at her new surroundings, it was love at first sight. The flatland South Carolina girl was in the mountains, and they would be her home for the next seventy years. At breakfast, in the dining room, she met other faculty members. One of the teachers was Grady Miller, who had just returned after serving in France during World War I. He would later be her husband and my father.

During the eleven years they were married, my mother and father spent less than two years in a house, and they never owned one. Most of the time, they lived in a small apartment on campus. I was seventeen days old when my father died suddenly from cerebral meningitis in March 1932. He left his wife and two children no land, no home, no furniture, and hardly any material possessions. An insurance policy provided $1,000. He also left $90 in cash, but expenses and an old debt Mother paid more than exhausted that.

Not far from where I was born, a creek flows from the foot of Double Knobs Mountain down through dense laurel thickets, pastures, and the old baseball diamond. It finally joins Brasstown Creek and then flows into the Hiawassee River and ultimately into the Gulf of Mexico. In this creek, swiftly flowing, clear mountain water polished thousands of beautiful rocks—shades of brown, gold, and amber. No one but a penniless artist like my mother would have dreamed in 1932 of using those rocks to build a house.

The creek ran through the property of a good friend. The friend was a little surprised by Mother's idea, but she readily agreed to let the recent widow have all the rocks she wanted. So, through summer 1932, my mother waded in the cold mountain water selecting rock after rock and piling them on the creek bank. The friend held me in her lap or laid me in the sun on the creek bank, and my six-year-old sister Jane played nearby. Hour after hour, day in and day out, a determined thirty-nine-year-old widow, trained as an artist at the Art Students League in New York, waded and stooped and lifted and carried.

The carefully selected stones were heaped on a wooden sled and pulled to the nearest dirt road, where on Saturday a truck owned by the college carried them to a field that was as close to the campus as Mother could buy for $200. The soil on the lot next to a rough dirt road was saturated with rocks and smothered by broomsedge. The old fence that surrounded it was matted with honeysuckle.

Labor was cheap because of the Great Depression. Men would work for a dollar or two a day. My mother drew her own plans, explained to the builders that she had only about $700, and instructed them to build until that was used up. The money lasted long enough to get the rocks laid, a roof on, the windows in, and one room finished. Everything else was left as was: naked rafters, sub-flooring, and a stairwell that was more like a ladder. There was no bathroom and no plumbing. The first night we lived in the room that was finished, a stray dog came in and ate the butter out of a dish.

The house stayed very much that way until I finished high school. One time we put a brooder in a corner of the living room and raised chickens in it. The mountains could get cold during wintertime, and a solitary fireplace provided heat until I was almost out of grammar school, when we began to enjoy the comfort of a wood heater. To this day, warmth is a luxury to me that I don't expect others to understand.

I remember wishing as a child that my mother was more like other mothers—mothers who were not muscular, whose hands were not gnarled, who did not work from daylight until dark, who got their house chores done and sat on the front porch. My mother never *sat* anywhere! She was always on the go, doing something, usually at a fast trot.

From my earliest childhood, Mother was selected to help at the polls, whether it was a state or local election. I think this was done for two reasons: it was well known she needed the money, and, just as important, she was one of the few that both warring political factions in our community trusted. So this, too, became a part of my boyhood memories—my mother's spending every election day and into the night at the "law house," as the little one-room structure was called.

All elections in Towns County generated incredible competition. I remember huddling in a corner during the "count out" as I listened to my mother call "tally" each time five votes were counted for a candidate. I also remember the politeness with which these combative, whiskered, overall-wearing men—some red-eyed from a few election-day drinks of moonshine—treated my mother, the only female in their hardened group.

With this beginning, it was probably inevitable my mother would herself become a candidate. She served on the Young Harris City Council for more than twenty-five years. She usually was the treasurer or clerk, which meant that she collected the town taxes and, later, when Young Harris got city water, the water bills.

Those bills were usually paid at the "law house" on a certain day, but most people preferred to drop by our house to make payments. A young lad, living alone with his mother and sister, learned much from such an experience. One lesson was that when a taxpayer paid his taxes, he usually had some choice comments on how that hard-earned money was to be spent. That's one thing that hasn't changed, even if politicians these days are afflicted with amnesia on the subject.

My mother was always elected without opposition, a fact that was almost unheard of in Towns County. She was elected mayor twice, one of the few lady mayors in Georgia. Earlier, she had been selected as the first woman to serve on a jury in Towns County. Many people, especially during the time a woman was an opponent in my first race for lieutenant governor, have asked what I think about liberated women and, especially, women in politics. I have always replied, "Frankly, I've never known anything else."

That also held true with the woman I married. Not only was I born a Democrat, I married a Democrat who was born a Democrat, as were her parents. From her earliest years, Shirley, even more than I, understood and lived by the curious code of mountain politics. She was raised in a place even more isolated and rural than the little village in which I grew up. Rail Cove, Cherokee County, North Carolina, is near the little town of Andrews, deep in the Great Smokey Mountains. My village is about four miles across; Shirley's cove is about one hundred yards wide. Four families lived there in her youth. A little creek covered on each side with ferns and mountain laurel runs through a lush dense forest of hemlocks and hardwoods. The mountains that rise up on each side are so steep they almost form a perfect V. Nantahala Gorge is only a few miles away. Nantahala is a Cherokee word meaning "land of the midday sun." In other words, only when the sun is straight up in the sky can it shine into those narrow crevices.

For many years, to get in and out of the cove you took a narrow footpath or drove a truck up the creek bed. Shirley's family first lived in a little three-room house that an elderly couple had just moved out of. When they moved in, they found a big mother hog living behind the "cook stove" in the kitchen. Whenever we visited Shirley's mother and the house was a little cluttered, right up to the day she died she would laugh and say, "At least there's not a sow in the kitchen."

Over the years, thanks to the sweat of several brows, it became a working farm with all the chores and hard living that went with it. That little house has been renovated time and time again, and we often spend time there when visiting her large extended family living nearby.

In that cove, in that Carver House, Franklin Delano Roosevelt was the patron saint who had saved the family from Herbert Hoover and the Republican depression. In that family circle, Harry Truman walked on water and they preferred erudite Adlai Stevenson, a man with whom they had little in common, over the military hero Dwight Eisenhower. I remember Shirley's father once replying to a Republican friend who had gone to hear Eisenhower make a speech and came back bragging that 5,000 people were there, "That's nothing. When Hoover was president, I saw that many chasing a rabbit." Luke Carver's family voted "straight Democrat" with no questions asked.

Over the years, I've tried to analyze those strong feelings. Of course, as I have mentioned, it went back to Andrew Jackson and the frontier, to the divisions brought on by secession and the Civil War, and, of course, to FDR who, to hear some tell it, invented electricity. But with Shirley's mother, "Bea," it was much deeper than all these historical reasons. She was part Cherokee Indian, as many were in the area, and at an early age was adopted and raised by a childless couple in Andrews. Later, she would look after them with the greatest of care through their years of old age and until their deaths. Bea had the heart and soul of a caring social worker. She would take in not only relatives but other needy, down-on-their-luck folks, and invite them to live in the already crowded little house. She'd explain to her family, "If there's room in the heart, there's room in the home" . . . and she'd set another plate at the table. A German immigrant lived in town and when World War II came along he was sent away somewhere for confinement, much as the Japanese-Americans were on the West Coast. Bea prepared a supper for him the night before he left. Few African-Americans lived in Andrews in the 1940s. When they visited white people, they knocked at the back door. But not at Bea Carver's; they came through the front door and sat with everyone else.

So, she is why I never laugh at mother-in-law jokes. I adored Bea. She was one of the best people I've ever known, truly one of God's good and faithful servants.

As for Shirley's father, he was straight out of central casting. His name was Luke and he looked like a Luke. Like in the movie, he held a "cool hand." A legendary lawman, he wore a Stetson hat but seldom carried a gun. He didn't have to. His eyes and slow, firm drawl were enough to get someone headed in the direction he wanted them to move. Sheriffs from nearby counties would get him to go with them when faced with a particularly bad or dangerous situation. Shirley's boyfriends were scared to death of him.

Most of the time, Luke was a deputy sheriff, but for a few years in the 1950s, he was the "high sheriff," as they called it, and the family lived in the bottom of the county jail. It was next door to the courthouse where, as a little girl, Shirley went with her daddy during "court week" to sit on the hard benches. The proceedings mesmerized her. Only the lawyers, all males, wore suits and ties, and it was not lost on the little girl the respect these "special" men showed her father.

Sometimes Luke took time off from law enforcement and its low pay in order to "follow construction," as it was called. He worked on the Lincoln Tunnel, the St. Lawrence Waterway, and the Hoover Dam and helped build missile sites in Nevada. An explosives expert, he took great pride in his ability to "blow up just what I wanted to blow up."

He was also a great poker player, a voracious reader, and a storyteller. He once explained economics to his new, college-educated son-in-law this way: "Socialism is when you own two cows and have to give one to your neighbor. Communism is when the government owns both the cows and gives you a little of the milk. Capitalism is when you own two cows, sell one, and buy a bull."

The Carver family managed a busy farm operation in Rail Cove. Shirley had a younger brother and sister, Bill and Jane. Everyone was responsible for certain chores. They owned mules and horses as well as more than a dozen brood cows that in spring birthed calves the family herded for fifteen miles over the mountain to graze on federal land. Four times a year, they hatched a thousand little chicks, raised them, and sold most as fryers. Each spring they plowed and planted crops in the small but rich fertile valley. Then they gathered and canned or stored the results of their labor in the smokehouse and root cellar. Shirley was driving a farm tractor when she was thirteen. She helped her daddy deliver calves and doctor the farm animals and as many as a dozen dogs that were used for hunting bear, fox, possums, coons, and rabbits.

I gained my first approval from Luke with a lucky shot one snowy day, hitting a running rabbit being chased by a pack of beagles. But the approval fell somewhat when later in the year I almost gave out on him while digging a groundhog out of a deep burrow where the dogs had chased it.

Shirley has always had the toughness of her father and the empathy and heart of her mother. About the best combination anyone could have, I'd say. One of our neighbors once said of her, "Shirley Miller could make a living on a flat rock."

Young Harris, Georgia in the 1950s.

She's a natural caretaker. As a teenager she regularly took medicine and provisions such as radio batteries to her grandfather, Jack "Pa" Carver, who lived without electricity and most other comforts of civilization far back in the Snowbird Mountains on West Buffalo Branch. The road was so bad, especially in the winter, she'd have to park the pickup a mile or more away and walk in. Most of the time, she'd travel alone, but once when "Pa" was having a "puny spell," her aunt went with her on a cold and icy February day. They found him sicker than anyone thought, so they decided to spend the night. He got worse and, in the middle of the night, he died. By the light of a kerosene lamp and a fireplace, they put coins on Pa Carver's eyes and tied a bandana around his head to pull his mouth shut. Then, holding hands, they sat by his bed and waited until daylight to go get Luke.

ELECTED A DEMOCRAT

I got my first taste of actually running for office in 1958. I was twenty-six, and along with first taste came first lesson: There is no such thing as apathy in mountain elections. Every voter attaches considerable value to a vote, and he or she expects you to work just as hard for a vote as you would for anything else of great value.

That year, three seats came available on the Towns County Democratic Executive Committee. It was a small but powerful group of fifteen people. In those days, it nominated the Democratic candidates for office, rather than have them run in primaries. The system was sort of like preventative medicine in that it evolved as a way to avoid the hot conflicts that developed in primaries, then carried over to the November general elections without giving the primary wounds time to heal. Both parties nominated that way in Towns County.

I stood outside the "law house" all day and asked Democrats to vote for me for one of the three seats. At this time, I was still a graduate student at the University of Georgia in Athens but took the day off to go home for the primary election in September. All of

Georgia's constitutional officers were running, including a race for governor.

The names of the candidates for the county committee were not on the ballot, so I had to persuade the voter to write my name in, if so inclined. I had been off in the Marine Corps for three years and at the University of Georgia for two more, so I had not been around Young Harris for a while. Mostly, I'd just greet and ask how they had been. They wanted to know about the children and how Shirley was. Looking back, I can't remember anyone expressing great surprise at my brazen candidacy, and many old friends came by after voting to tell me they had "put one in" for me. It was a good feeling and one to which I knew I could become easily addicted. It was four o'clock before I realized I had not had lunch. A little more than two hundred voters went to the polls in Young Harris that day, and I got forty-something write-in votes, barely enough to be one of the county committee members.

I was elected to the committee, and before I could turn around, I found myself being pushed by some to seek the nomination for state representative. Problem was, the new committee wouldn't be doing the voting. When the old committee met, I lost the nomination by one vote. I had a hard time understanding why the old committee nominated instead of the one just elected, but I was told that was the way the chairman had ordered it. So, I had both my first taste and my first lesson in Towns County politics.

Just as strange as the way I lost an election was the way I won one. Later that year, I was elected mayor of Young Harris. The election was held one Saturday afternoon while I had gone to Athens to attend a University of Georgia football game. I didn't even know an election was going on. When I got back from the game about dark, Doyle Bryson, my Uncle Hoyle's brother and a council member who had helped hold the election, walked up the hill to the college-owned house we lived in and said, "A-okay, Mayor. You got ninety-eight votes."

Here is what had happened while I was gone. Mayor was an office I had not really thought about because city government was my mother's area and I knew two Millers in it would be one too many. My mother had volunteered earlier that morning to retire from the town council when someone had mentioned they ought to have some "young blood" on the council.

Now, the job description for mayor of Young Harris sometimes went beyond the boundaries of a similar job in most places. Young Harris did not have a police department, and every once in a while the mayor had to serve as a law enforcement officer. When he was sworn in to the office, he was given not only the seal and books of the city, but, in case a town policeman was ever hired, a .38 Special and a blackjack. When they were handed to me after I was sworn in, I startled the new council when I slapped the blackjack on the table and said, "This meeting of the Young Harris City Council will come to order." There was no gavel.

Once a hot-rodder, with his dual exhausts and gutted mufflers, made a nuisance of himself by speeding back and forth in the little town. When I tried to approach his car to ask him to stop, he would "burn rubber" and speed off with squealing tires. He finally got so brazen he did a "wheel-job" in front of our house while I was pitching baseball in the yard. I didn't have the pistol so I used the only weapon I had and with my better-than-average shortstop's arm, I threw the baseball at him. It hit the back window with a thud and the smart aleck sped off with a window broken by a mayor who had taken the law into his own hands (or arm).

I began to think seriously about running for the State Senate seat in 1960. Young, idealistic, in a hurry, I was unhappy with the leadership of the Democratic Party. One man controlled the entire county. His name was W. K. (Kaiser) Dean. He was the chairman of the Towns County Democratic Party and had been a state senator and representative. With his big belly, suspenders, and foghorn voice, he was the epitome of the political boss. Although the county was divided equally between Democrats and Republicans, it never crossed my mind that I could switch and become a Republican and run against him that way. I was a Democrat, born a Democrat, and we'd fight it out within the party.

My first step was to go to Dr. Charles Clegg, president of Young Harris College, and ask if I could make the race. In retrospect, I think the president considered me a good teacher even though I had been back home barely a year and he must have figured I had little chance of changing the local political structure. He took the fatherly approach of allowing me to get "running" out of my system so then I could get on with the business of being a professional educator. At any rate, he gave his approval to my candidacy, and in January 1960 at the age of twenty-seven I announced that I would run for the State Senate.

The way I was taught to prepare for an election was to take the voting list for each precinct and go over it with a knowledgeable person who lived in that district. When I eventually represented that area in the Senate, I knew each citizen so well I could do it without help. I would go down the list putting plus signs by the names of those known to favor my candidacy, minus signs by those who opposed it, and small circles by those whose views were unknown. Known as "floaters," these were the ones to whom I would pay particular attention.

The primary was held in April, and I worked relentlessly during the cold winter days and nights. An old-timer had told me, "Politics is like fighting rats. You've got to go at it night and day." I did. I got up before daybreak to visit the early-rising mountain families around Owl Creek, Gum Log, Scataway, Bugscuffle, Bearmeat, and the other isolated communities throughout the county. I'd be back at the college by nine o'clock to teach my first class.

There was an old custom that if you woke up a man at night, it would emphasize to him just how important you thought his vote was. I woke up dozens. I'd always carry a gun on those excursions because feelings ran high and I traveled alone often on dark, lonely, dirt-rutted roads.

I didn't even bother to go to the homes of known Republicans who would not vote in the Democratic Primary, but I visited every Democratic household in the county, some of them time and time again. Other candidates had always visited only one or two key men in each precinct, who, like old ward leaders, were relied on to get the vote out and carry the precincts for their candidates. They were good men, usually the heads of large families, and took pride in their political abilities. They controlled the patronage, which usually consisted of a few state jobs with the Highway, Revenue, and Game and Fish Departments.

Georgia's county unit system was still in effect in those days. The system worked like the electoral college. It was a unique system that had been used in the Democratic primary since 1877 and was tantamount to election. I was in my first term as state senator in 1962 when it was declared unconstitutional by the U.S. Supreme Court and the "one-man, one-vote" became the basis for all elections.

The way it had worked up until then was that each of Georgia's 159 counties (more than any other state except Texas) had twice as many unit votes as it had representatives in the lower house of the Legislature. The eight largest counties, which had three representatives each, had six unit votes. The next thirty counties, with two representatives each, had four unit votes each. The remaining 121 counties, with one representative each, had two unit votes each. Obviously, if one could do well in the rural counties, it little mattered how one did in the urban areas. Eugene Talmadge, elected governor four separate times under the system, used to brag he didn't want to carry a county with a streetcar in it.

At the time it finally was declared illegal, Georgia's largest county, Fulton, had a population of 566,326 and paid 25 percent of all the taxes. Yet Georgia's three smallest counties, with a combined total population of 6,980, could equal its influence. Towns County at that time was 151st in size with a population of about 4,500.

I did not ignore the key leaders in each precinct, but I did not rely solely on them either. In fact, a few were automatically on my side, not because they were for me but because they were against my opponent. I've found that this is the case in every election; there are people who don't vote for you but vote against your opponent. It counts just the same.

I was young and looked even younger. I was less than four years out of the Marine Corps and still wore the closely clipped hairstyle. Shirley cut it. I'll never forget an old-timer looking at my high, tight "white wall" and snorting, "You'll never be elected to anything, son, with your hair cut like that."

But the biggest obstacle was that my opponent totally controlled the election machinery, and I quickly learned how important this was in a rural county. To begin with, my opponent, Kaiser Dean, was chairman of the party, and the secretary was his right-hand man. When my candidacy became known, it suddenly became impossible for me to get in touch with either of them in order to qualify and pay the qualifying fee. Finally, one morning while it was still dark, I got up, took my $150 check, and drove to the secretary's house. I knocked on the door before daylight and handed the startled man standing there in his long underwear my qualifying fee. This gave me the idea of what I was up against, but it was nothing compared to what I later ran into when every single person who worked at each polling place was appointed by my opponent.

Towns County had eight precincts that since have been reduced to four. At that time, some voting was done outdoors at what was called the "law ground" or in a barn. They used the back of a truck in Gum Log, and when the inevitable fight broke out among drunken observers, the election-holders simply drove the "voting place" down the road and away from the fracas. Often the drunks would follow and they'd just move the truck another half-mile or so. Sometimes by the end of the day, when the polls closed, the truck and the election holders would be a mile or two from where they started.

Tate City was the smallest precinct in Towns County. Far back in an isolated cove, one could get to it only by driving over the mountain to Rabun County and then coming into it on an old rutted road from that side of the mountain. There were fourteen votes in Tate City, all in one family. In close elections they would be divided; in others the front-runner would get all of them. In my first race they hedged; I carried Tate City eight to six. They were all Democratic votes, however, and Republicans didn't even bother to campaign in Tate City. They would bring in the totals whenever all fourteen voted, and it was common occurrence to hear the returns from Tate City soon after lunch on election day.

Prior to each election, I paid a courtesy visit to Tate City to visit Arthur Young, who was the head of the clan. He jokingly referred to himself as the mayor of Tate City. He lived in a 150-year-old log cabin with a front porch that was fenced in to keep the dogs and animals out, not in. There was no electricity, and the outdoor toilet was built over a mountain stream nearby.

The reason I always enjoyed visiting Arthur was because he was a great fiddle player. If you hit him just right, he would drag out a couple of homemade fiddles and play a few numbers—old tunes he had played all of his life, most of which did not even have names. He would sometimes stop in the middle of one and say, "I need a little lubrication to limber up my elbow." Then he would either fetch out a jar of moonshine or put the fiddle up, depending upon the encouragement his audience gave him.

The hard work paid off—not just my hard work, but that of dozens of friends who believed in me. I remember to this day the overwhelming sense of gratitude I felt at seeing "haulers" bringing in people to the polls who, because they were riding with my friends, I knew would be voting for me.

When the ballots were counted late that night, I won by 151 votes. I left the Hiawassee courthouse that was filled with grizzled mountaineers and their stories of fights, of vote-buying, and of all the other shenanigans that had happened that day in their precincts and returned to my home, where a large number of my fresh-faced college students gathered outside the house and sang "For He's a

Jolly Good Fellow." My twenty-four-year-old wife and my four- and five-year-old sons looked on in amazement, wondering what I had gotten us into.

Although no law required me to do so, and it was unheard of, the next week I published an itemized account of my campaign contributions and expenses in the county paper. The campaign cost came to a grand total of $419, of which my friends contributed $137.50.

GOVERNED AS A DEMOCRAT

5

When I finally ran for governor in 1990, I had knocked around in
Georgia politics and government for thirty years. Sixteen of those
years had been spent as lieutenant governor. Unlike some states
where that office is a meaningless appendage, in Georgia it was a
position with muscle. The lieutenant governor presided as president
of the Senate. He appointed all committees, all chairmen and
subcommittee chairmen, and all conference committee members
and assigned all bills to committees. Only in Texas was the office
more powerful. Over time I became good friends with two of its
lieutenant governors, Bill Hobby and Bob Bullock, who I admired
for their effective use of their office to achieve good things for their
state.

It was a good job and I liked it, obviously. I didn't mind at all the
kidding that I had decided to be "lieutenant governor for life." I
especially enjoyed the budgetary process and the annual fights we
'had with the House under the stern and dominate leadership of
Speaker Tom Murphy, a yellow dog, New Deal Democrat, who, by
the time he was defeated by a Republican in 2002, had served as

Speaker some twenty-eight years, longer than anyone in the country.

While I always helped the governors with their programs, I often pushed my own agenda, such as the Mountain Protection Act that provided for building restrictions on the higher mountain ridges, removing the state sales tax from food, pushing open meetings legislation and tort reform, and limiting the amount of money that could be raised and spent for political campaigns. Cutting taxes, protecting the environment, and limiting money in elections—I had been fighting for these long before I came to Washington.

I was first elected lieutenant governor in 1974 and then three more times by wide margins. I never spent more than $200,000, never hired any consultants or pollsters or ran a single television ad. The campaigns were built solely on personal contacts around the state laboriously driving from one community to another, hitting the mill shifts, courthouses, civic clubs, and local media outlets.

Coming on the heels of my job with Governor Jimmy Carter as executive director of the Democratic Party of Georgia and as a staff person to two other governors, I had accumulated a wealth of contacts and friends as I traveled into every county and city over and over from one end of Georgia to the other. That placed me in good stead in the four races for lieutenant governor, but I knew that to be elected governor would require more than running a race out of my own hip pocket, as I had been accused of doing for so many years. So, in 1989 I attended more than two hundred separate fundraisers all over the state and raised my first million dollars, usually at $25-a-person events. That allowed me to hire a consultant just like the big boys did. I had begun to follow the career of James Carville, a wisecracking consultant with an accent even stranger than mine. He had helped Bob Casey, once called "the third loss from Holy Cross" because of his inability to win elections, to win an election as governor of Pennsylvania. Casey's nickname sounded about as bad as "Zig Zag" Zell, which I had lived with since the 1980 U.S. Senate race against Herman Talmadge. Another Democratic candidate in that race, Norman Underwood, had called me that. He later became one of my best friends, and when I was governor I appointed him the chairman of my Judicial Nominating Committee that made recommendations to me for judgeships. I also had watched Carville win a U.S. Senate race in New Jersey with Frank Lautenberg over college football's Heisman Trophy icon and West Point legend Pete Dawkins, a most attractive candidate. But the thing that really sold me was the win in Kentucky where with Carville's help, Wallace Wilkinson, an unknown businessman, rode the promise of a lottery to victory as governor.

I had already decided I wanted to make the lottery an issue in my race—not because I liked gambling, but because I had some things I desperately wanted to accomplish in education. Having worked closely with the budget and knowing long-range revenue projections, I realized Georgia's new governor would be faced with drastically shrinking revenues because of the coming recession. The cupboard would be bare.

So, I called James Carville, whom I had met in 1980 when he worked for Raymond Strother. The first words out of his mouth were "I knew someday you would call me." A couple of weeks later I met with James and Paul Begala for breakfast one morning at La Colline in Washington, D.C., and hired them on the spot. I didn't realize it at the time, but they had gone four months without a paycheck and needed me about as much as I needed them.

We made a good team. We all loved baseball, country music, and politics. We all three knew what cracklin' cornbread was. And we all hated like hell to lose. Oh yes, there were times when the Marine from the mountains would clash with the Marine from the bayou, but overall we got along. I often didn't know what Carville was saying, but we all knew he was in charge. This was different from my other five statewide races in which I was the campaign manager, press secretary, and chief fund-raiser all in one. Carville had a unique ability to see around corners, and Begala had a unique ability to translate what James saw around those corners. I had

With James Carville and Paul Begala.

already chosen the basis of my campaign: (1) a lottery for two special education initiatives—a merit scholarship for college students and a statewide pre-kindergarten program; (2) the removal of sales tax from groceries (which I had been trying to do for years); and (3) a Marine-type boot camp for young first offenders. Other planks were added to this program along the way, but these three remained at the heart of what I called "the Georgia that can be."

I think we learned a lot from each other. I know I learned a lot from James and Paul, and I know for certain I could not have been elected governor without them. I faced formidable primary opposition: Andrew Young, former Atlanta mayor, U.S. ambassador, and congressman; state Senator Roy Barnes, a brilliant lawyer; and Representative Lauren ("Bubba") McDonald, the candidate of my nemesis Speaker Murphy; and in the general election, Johnny Isakson, a highly respected Republican leader.

They were all quality candidates and quality people. Later I appointed Isakson as chairman of the State Board of Education and Democrat McDonald to the Public Service Commission. Barnes was elected governor in 1998 and appointed me to the U.S. Senate after the death of Paul Coverdell in July 2000. Young, of course, continues to hold the most prestigious position of all of us by just being Andy Young. Andy and I had worked closely together for years and during the campaign to have Atlanta host the Olympic Games in 1996. It was Andy, more than any other single person, who swung the votes of the Third World countries in Atlanta's favor. It was also Andy who, after the Olympic Park bombing, brought everyone back together again with one of his greatest speeches.

As anticipated, when I took office in January 1991, Georgia and the nation were in a recession. State revenues had slipped below the level of appropriations, and the reserves were completely empty. Even so, I refused to raise taxes to bring the budget into balance. Instead, I put on the green eyeshade and immersed myself in the budget beginning at seven o'clock the morning after the election. Fortunately, I had been part of the budgetary process for years and knew the numbers pretty well. I had realized a full year before that if I had any hope of realizing my big dreams for education, I'd have to pull a rabbit out of a hat. That is why early in the campaign I had turned to the lottery as the hat. The other candidates quickly disavowed it, as I knew they would. I had the issue all to myself. The conventional wisdom was that I had committed political suicide. In that first conversation with James, when I mentioned my lottery for education idea, he immediately shot back, "It will poll 67-33 percent, but that 33 percent will beat you to death." How right he was about those who opposed it.

They were brutal and they were relentless. They were my neighbors, family, and fellow church members. They fell into three categories: those who sincerely believed that the lottery was immoral and that I was wrong to suggest it; those who cared nothing about its morality but thought I was a devious and lying politician who would never use the money for the programs I promised; and supporters who felt sure I was making a huge mistake that would end my career. I told the first group I respected their opinion, the second group that it would be used for merit scholarships and pre-kindergarten and not be put in the general fund as Florida had done, and the third group, "You gotta trust me. I'm sure I'm right." (Although sometimes late at night, I wondered. After all, Georgia was the buckle of the Bible Belt.) The most vehement opposition came from the Atlanta newspapers and the Georgia Council on Moral and Civic Concerns. The latter called the lottery "voodooism and paganism." The newspaper predicted the lottery commission would become an "out-of-sight place for politicians to employ their dim-witted cousins and down and out brothers-in-law."

After a runoff with Young and a tough general election with Isakson, I was elected by 54 percent. But I still would have a difficult time getting the bill through the Legislature, even though it had been the main plank in my successful campaign.

A big, rawboned Irishman with an unlit cigar in the corner of his mouth and an LBJ Stetson on his balding head, Tom Murphy has been a legend in Georgia politics and state legislative politics across the nation for more than a quarter-century. We both had come to the Georgia Legislature in the same year, 1961, the Navy veteran to the House and this Marine veteran to the Senate. Our paths would cross thousands of times over the next forty years—and our wills would clash time and time again.

The presiding officers of the two legislative bodies in any state often have differences of opinions; that's natural. But we set the record. We knew how to push each other's buttons, and we'd fight viciously. Sometimes we would make up, swear we were going to get along better, and after a drink or three, sing a duet of "Your Cheating Heart" that would make the dogs howl. And then the next day, or the next week, we'd be at it again, he referring to me as the "extinguished lieutenant governor" and I calling his House "Murphy's Mausoleum."

Our first big fight occurred the first day I was in office as lieutenant governor. It was over open meetings for conference committees. I was for it; he was against it. The last big battle was almost twenty-five years later over welfare reform, when I was governor and he was still Speaker. Some amateur psychologists have called it a "love-hate" relationship, and looking back, I think they were right. I felt very close to his son, a fine lawyer I would appoint as a superior court judge. The Speaker, on the other hand, felt close to Shirley and she to him for some reason. Over the years, more than once he has acknowledged that "we would have killed each other if it hadn't been for 'Miz Shirley.'"

He had defeated my first attempt to pass a lottery in 1990 and had his own handpicked candidate running for governor. So, when I was elected, I went to him immediately and said, "Mr. Speaker, I might can get elected without you, but I can't govern without you." We shook hands and swore we'd work better together, and we did. He and Lt. Gov. Pierre Howard were of immense help during the budget crunch.

Speaker Murphy had blocked the lottery in the House in the session of 1990. But after I won the election with it as my main issue, he said he would take hands off and let the House work its will. For help, I turned to another respected member of the Georgia House. Denmark Groover had been a Marine pilot in World War II in the famous "Black Sheep Squadron" commanded by the colorful Gregory "Pappy" Boyington. Back in the wild and wooly days in 1962 at the height of the controversy over reapportionment, and with time running out on the closing evening of the session, he startled everyone by suddenly running off the floor of the House and up into the gallery, where he leaned far over the rail, holding on with one hand and almost falling off, tore the huge clock off the wall, and sent it smashing loudly to the floor of the House. It was a miracle someone didn't get hurt. It failed to stop the reapportionment bill, and "Denny," as his friends called him, got his photo in *Time*.

Denny and I also had served together for years. Sometimes he would oppose my legislation, but at other times we worked closely together. On this occasion he came down to the governor's office and volunteered to help me. He told me why. He said, "I've always said there are three things men are always going to do. They are going to drink liquor, they are going to run around with women, and they are going to gamble. The stomach is going to take care of the first, old age can take care of the second, but ain't nothing going to stop them from gambling. So as far as I'm concerned, a lottery is just fine with me."

I had some able floor leaders in the House, but we knew we would need Denny's help. The lottery passed the Senate easily, but the debate went on for some time in the House. Denny waited to be the last speaker. Everyone knew the vote would be close, and the members were anxious to hear what this revered member would have to say. He first reminded the House members that he had supported their colleague "Bubba" McDonald in the governor's race against me, and then said, "The Constitution of this state says that all government of right emanates from the people. And this man had the guts to propose a lottery and he was the only one that did. He ran on it and he was elected on it. The people wanted an opportunity to vote on it themselves. Are we going to give them that opportunity to see it, or are we going to take our own personal prejudices and political fears and kill it here?" The resolution was adopted by the House with 126 "ayes" and 51 "nays," only six votes more than was needed. When it was put directly to the people two years later in a statewide referendum, it eked out a 52-48 margin.

When I finally completed all the procedures for my first budget, I ended up cutting state expenditures by a total of $944 million, raising hunting and fishing and driver's license fees for the first time in decades, and abolishing about 5,000 state jobs over a period of three years. But it was this disciplined approach to state finances that enabled the Miller Administration to achieve its goals while later simultaneously reducing taxes by $883 million through three tax cuts—two income tax cuts and, at last, the removal of the state sales tax from groceries.

The central purpose of my administration was to prepare Georgia for the twenty-first century, and strengthening education was at the heart of that task. Over and over, I told the people I wanted to create a culture of greater expectations in Georgia, so that students would not ask "whether" to go to college or technical school, but "where." I also wanted to make government leaner and more efficient, make the streets safer, protect the environment, and give Georgia's citizens a tax break every time they sat down to eat a meal.

In my inaugural speech, I dedicated my administration to "real Georgians—the farmer who planted his own crops and baled his own hay, the small businesswoman who stayed open late and called her customers by their first names, the entrepreneur who built a better mousetrap or microchip, the senior citizen who feared having to choose between eating and heating her house, the young family struggling to pay for daycare and save for college at the same time, and to every Georgian who worked and saved and sometimes came up a little short at the end of the month." It was these salt-of-the-earth citizens whose lives I wanted to touch in tangible ways that they could understand and appreciate.

To move an agenda, a governor cannot be shy and there are fights he or she cannot afford to lose, especially early in an administration. Six months into my administration, I got into one of those. I was the chief executive, I had been elected, and now I wanted to name my own highway director. This is difficult in Georgia because the transportation board is a constitutionally independent body that jealously guards its powers. Sound familiar to one's Washington ears? I wanted a change because over the years, the department had become too powerful and insensitive not only to the general public but to local officials and legislators who had to deal with it. The department had become a separate branch of government. The last governor had tried to clip their wings and had failed. Not only did I want a change, but the Speaker of the House and lieutenant governor did also. They too had become fed up with the bulldozing ways of the commissioner and the board.

So I invited this "autonomous" board to lunch at the Governor's Mansion with the three of us. After feeding them well, I got to the point that we all knew was coming. "Gentlemen, we need a change of leadership over at the DOT." I then asked them to fire the commissioner and support another one, Wayne Shackleford, who I had waiting in another room. The chairman responded, "Governor, we appreciate your position, but we don't even know Mr. Shackleford and would like more time to consider this. And we can't say anymore about it than that today."

I then replied that we had the media gathered in a hall outside for an announcement and we were willing to wait until they made a decision. I continued, "You say you don't know Mr. Shackleford very well. Well, gentlemen, you must not know Zell Miller very well. You should know that I'm a little crazy. If you think for a minute that I'm going to let you destroy my administration, then you're dead wrong. And I've got the tools at my disposal to prevent you from doing that."

I then reminded them of how the budget process begins and ends with the governor. "I have a line-item veto and I can slash your budget to the bone. Now I know your big money is dedicated by law from motor fuel taxes. Well, look at these two presiding officers of the Senate and the House. We can undedicate it and we will if you make us. We can also set up a completely new board and strip you of your power and your funds. You may still exist but you won't have any power. Your board membership will be meaningless."

I was getting hot under the collar and they knew it. I continued, "Reapportionment is coming up and we can also redraw the lines of your districts. We can put two of you in the same district and let you fight it out."

You could have cut the tension in the air with a knife. Lt. Gov. Howard broke the silence. "Governor, why don't you step outside and let me and the Speaker talk with them." We had prearranged this and I left. Then the Speaker told them, "The governor's not kidding and we're with him." Then the two of them left the room, after saying, "Think about it." In fifteen minutes, they called us back in. They told us the present commissioner would resign and that Mr. Shackleford would be interviewed immediately, and they also would stop pushing for an increase in the motor fuel tax. We then held our press conference and announced those results. The next day a reporter asked me if I thought this situation would make my department heads afraid of me. I replied, "I hope it does."

To make sure other constitutional boards would not be able to thwart my programs, sometimes when I appointed a department head or board member I would ask him to give me a signed but undated letter of resignation. I never had one refuse, but I never used it. With it in my drawer, I didn't have to.

But I also had defeats along the way, most notably my attempt to change Georgia's flag. The flag flap almost did me in, as it later would Governor David Beasley, who tried to change it in South Carolina, and Governor Roy Barnes, who did get the Georgia flag changed only to go down in defeat over it in 2002.

In 1993, I gave it my best shot. I called the legislative leadership in and made my pitch. They said I was crazy. I called the leaders of the business community in and they gave me a standing ovation, but as later events were to prove, that was about all. I'll never forget one important leader who minced no words in support. He was then Speaker of the House Newt Gingrich, who put out a statement of support from Washington. A survey showed 55 percent wanted to keep it, and calls ran 5-1 against changing it. But I plowed ahead and when the legislative session convened, I devoted most of my State of the State address to it.

I will never forget my great-grandfather, Brantley Bryan, who was wounded while fighting with Stonewall Jackson at Chancellorsville, then wounded again and more severely at Gettysburg in the same battle that took his brother's life. But I also cannot forget the millions of Georgians, my ancestors and yours, who also made sacrifices in other wars, both before and after the War Between the States . . . .

Georgia will be 260 years old next month. For forty-three of those years, we were a British colony. For eleven years, a sovereign state under the Articles of Confederation. For more than 200 years, a member of the United States. For four brief years—that's 1.5 percent of our state's entire history—Georgia was a member of the Confederate States of America. Yet it is the Confederacy's most inflammatory symbol that dominates our flag today. We all know why. And it has nothing to do with the bravery of the Confederate troops . . . .

My all-time favorite movie is *To Kill A Mockingbird*—the Academy Award winner based on Harper Lee's story about life in the South in the early 1900s, with Gregory Peck as Atticus Finch, a lawyer raising two small children. In that movie's key scene, Atticus is defending a black man unjustly accused of rape, and a lynch mob tries to take justice into its own hands. As Atticus confronts the mob at the jailhouse door, his daughter, Scout, joins him and sees that the leader is someone she knows. And she calls him by name. "Hey, Mr. Cunningham. Remember me? You're Walter's daddy. Walter's a good boy. Tell him I said hello." After a dramatic pause, Mr. Cunningham turns and says to the mob, "Let's go, boys." A group bent on injustice was turned aside by one small girl who appealed to them as individuals. Well, my friends in this chamber, I know you. And I appeal to each of you as individuals—as fathers and mothers, as neighbors and friends, most of who were taught in Sunday school to "Do unto others as you would have them do unto you" . . . .

I then spoke to each of the different groups of the Legislature: leaders, veteran legislators, rising stars, Republicans, and freshmen.

Then Atlanta Mayor, Andrew Young visits the Georgia Senate just across the street from City Hall.

To the Republicans I said, "Republicans, believe it or not, I know you. I respect your traditions, and the rebel yell of the lost cause sounds especially harsh and awkward in your throats. Your vote on this issue will say much about where you aim to take the party of Lincoln in a changing state."

I ended by saying:

Since 1789 Georgia's motto has been "Wisdom, Justice, Moderation." There is nothing wise, just, or moderate in a flag that reopens old wounds and perpetuates old hatreds. Our battle-fields. Our graveyards. Our monuments. Important reminders of our history, both the proud and the painful. They will and always should be there. That's history. But our flag is a symbol—a symbol of what we stand for as a state. I want to see this state live by the words of George Washington to the sexton of the Rhode Island synagogue: "Ours is a government which gives to bigotry no sanction, to persecution no assistance." If you're truly proud of the South, if you're truly proud of this state, and all of its 260 years, if you look forward and want to play a significant part in what Georgia can become, then help me now to give bigotry no sanction, and persecution no assistance.

I failed to persuade. I just made them mad. I was like a kamikaze pilot who killed himself but didn't alter the war in the slightest.

The next year, in 1994, a wealthy Atlanta businessman, Republican Guy Millner, bankrolled his own campaign against me. By this time, Carville and Begala were new stars and busy in Washington. I selected Jim Andrews as my campaign manager. Brilliant and ornery, I consider Jim the best consultant working today. I would never have won without him. It was a tough year for Democratic incumbent governors; Mario Cuomo of New York and Ann Richards of Texas were both defeated, though considered charismatic and somewhat safe. I barely got by.

The economy had improved and the lottery was successful. I had two important goals—to launch a voluntary pre-kindergarten program for four-year-old children and to provide scholarships to students who maintained high grades. The lottery-funded pre-kindergarten program was successful beyond my greatest dreams. By the time I left office, 61,000 children were being served by that program each year at an annual cost of almost $218 million. Georgia is still today, ten years later, the only state in the nation with a full-time pre-kindergarten program.

HOPE scholarships are also unique to Georgia. HOPE stands for Helping Outstanding Pupils Educationally and provides financial assistance for college to students who graduate from a Georgia public or private high school with at least a B average. Those attending Georgia's public colleges or universities receive free tuition, paid mandatory fees, and a book allowance. Those attending private institutions in the state receive a scholarship of $3,000 a year. If they keep a B average, year by year, those benefits

The father of the HOPE Scholarship is congratulated by the father of the Pell Scholarship, U.S. Senator Claiborn Pell (D-RI).

continue through all four years. A Georgia high school graduate who is not a B student can enroll in a diploma-granting program at a technical institute on a HOPE scholarship. Funding pre-kindergarten and HOPE scholarships alone would have made the Georgia lottery a treasure for education. But lottery funds were also sufficient enough to appropriate $625 million for technology and $581 million for school construction during the Miller years.

These funds provided computers, satellite dishes, and other information technology for public school classrooms, media centers, colleges, universities, public libraries, and technical institutes. Training centers were created to give teachers the skills they needed to use the new technology. We linked all of the libraries of Georgia's thirty-four public colleges and universities and made it possible for any student in the University System to use the resources of all libraries at all institutions. Also, public libraries and technical institutes were linked to this massive online library, and they all had direct access to the Internet.

Technology is great, but I have always believed that the most effective way to improve education is to put better teachers in the classrooms. I believed the best way to do that was to increase teacher salaries at a faster pace than other states in order to attract more highly qualified teachers. Once we were out of the recession, I pursued that goal by giving teachers in public schools, the university system, and all technical institutes a 6 percent pay raise each year for four straight years. Georgia's salaries for teachers and professors went from seventh to the top in the Southeast. We also had a one-billion-dollar construction program for the university system's thirty-four institutions.

A major reason for my focus on education was to make sure that Georgia workers had the knowledge and training required for highly skilled jobs. Thus, Georgia's technical institutes were another important component of the educational delivery system. I felt this area of education needed a significant boost, including increased operating money and expanded facilities. By the time I left office, every Georgia citizen had access to technical education within a forty-five-minute driving distance from his or her residence.

The number of citizens who were illiterate or semi-literate handicapped Georgia's economic development effort, and one of many adult literacy initiatives was to locate at least one full-time adult literacy teacher with resources in every one of Georgia's 159 counties. This was Shirley's top priority as first lady, and she worked at it relentlessly.

I knew that a vibrant economy would provide a higher standard of living for all citizens. So I pushed for economic development to be incorporated into both the research and academic missions of the university system, and I insisted that these institutions work together and stop working at cross-purposes.

The Georgia Research Alliance embraced all six of Georgia's major research universities—public and private—in a unique part-

nership with each other and with the private sector. The Alliance
conducted practical applied research that would boost industry, and
we decided to concentrate on the three areas of telecommunica-
tions, biotechnology, and environmental technology. We also set up
the Traditional Industries Program to serve the research needs of
the three long-time manufacturing industries in Georgia—pulp and
paper, textile and apparel, and food processing.

Economic development was brought into the academic mission
of the University System as never before through the creation of
ICAPP, the Intellectual Capital Partnership Program, which focused
on workforce preparation for college-educated workers. Another
key element of economic development was the program "Quick
Start," where the state would actually train a company's employees
without cost. We also had strong trade and ports programs that
made Georgia a gateway to the world for the entire Southeast.

More than a million new citizens came to Georgia during the
eight years I was governor, making us fourth in numerical population growth and sixth in percentage growth during that period.
Many newcomers came because of the new jobs created in our state
during this time—an average of more than 2,000 new jobs per
week. Total personal income increased 68 percent, ranking Georgia
sixth among all states in income growth during that time. Georgia
moved from eleventh to tenth in population among all states and
for the first time received a AAA bond rating.

One of my most important initiatives had to do with welfare
reform, cutting the rolls in half and payments by more than $100
million. We then took those savings, added to them, and provided
transportation, childcare, GED education, treatment for drug abuse,
and other services needed to help welfare recipients become
productive citizens.

Runaway Medicaid growth was stopped dead in its tracks. Most
will tell you that it's impossible, but it can be done. In the ten years
before I took office, the Medicaid budget had increased 376 percent.
As governor, I decided to put on the brakes. I used a story I had told

a hundred times—so many in fact that the late Jerry Clower put it on one of his comedy albums and gave me credit for it. Here's an abbreviated version.

> Seems that a building caught fire in Young Harris and not having even a volunteer fire department back then, we all were just kind of standing around watching it go up in flames. When all of a sudden out of one of those hollows came this local character driving an old dilapidated pickup. He had his whole family with him, his wife, all the kids, and even Granny in the back. When he got the pickup to where we all were gathered just watching, he didn't stop but just drove the pickup right into the edge of the building. They all piled out and started stomping at the fire. Then, they had a couple of old blankets in the back of the truck and they started beating the blazes with them. Lo and behold, they got the fire out. Our mayor was there and said "Let's pass the hat for this brave man and his family." They took up $14.75. The mayor made a little speech: "Fuzz, this is the bravest thing we've ever seen in our little town. You're a hero and we want to show you our appreciation. By the way, how are you going to spend it?" Fuzz had lost a shoe and a sleeve of his shirt. One eyebrow was singed off. He took the money and answered, "Well, the first thing I'm going to do is get some brakes put on that pickup."

In ten years, a 376 percent increase! Way too much, so, even as we greatly expanded services to pregnant women and children, we put the brakes on. Through managed care and tougher fraud and abuse provisions, the increase during my last three years was less than 3 percent! This could be done on the federal level if we had the will to do it, for the system is filled with abuse and fraud that is beyond belief.

The protection of environmentally sensitive land was another high priority, and two initiatives dramatically expanded the natural land under state protection—Preservation 2000 and Rivercare 2000, with more than 110,000 acres purchased. Also, the Chattahoochee

River corridor, which had been designated one of the most abused rivers in the nation, was cleaned up.

We opened a record number of prison beds, more than 20,000, almost doubling the capacity when I took office. The additional bed capacity enabled me to end the practice in Georgia that had gone on for years of managing inmate population through the early release of criminals, and it also allowed me to implement my "two strikes" law for violent felons.

When I left office in January 1999, my administration received wonderful accolades about the job we had done. The *Atlanta Constitution,* always fair but not always in agreement with my policies, wrote in part, "In his foresight he has ushered the people of his native state to the brink of a new millennium well-prepared for whatever the future may bring." Of course, they thought, as I did, that I was through with politics. Their assessment next time I leave office will not be as positive.

This Democratic governor had done his best and, as promised, had plowed deep. But I also knew that it is history, not one's self and not one's contemporaries, that is the only judge of a man's real worth.

BUT NOT THIS KIND OF DEMOCRAT

6

Every Tuesday while the U.S. Senate is in session, the members of each party meet in a luncheon caucus to plan for the coming week, discuss strategy, and dog-cuss the other party. The Democratic senators meet in an ornate room just a few feet outside the Senate Chamber, in what is known as the Lyndon Baines Johnson room. It was in this room that the great majority leader moved his office in 1959 and liked it so well that he kept it when he became vice president. It remained his office until he became president in 1963. The room had originally been planned as the Senate library and is elaborately decorated with elegant fresco murals on the ceiling and walls designed by Constantino Brumidi, the great Italian artist who did the Capitol's rotunda.

A huge crystal chandelier dominates the room. Over in one corner, a big wooden box about three feet deep, eight feet wide, and twelve feet high served as LBJ's toilet because he didn't want to go out into the hallway to go to the rest room and be buttonholed by tourists and hangers-on. Not a modest man, Johnson would often take phone calls and dictate letters while sitting on the john. Today, a bronze plaque and a Norman Rockwell portrait of LBJ adorn one wall.

The luncheons begin at 12:30 and usually last until 2:00. We sat at tables of eight and the food was from the Senate dining room, one floor below. I usually had a bowl of soup, chicken salad with a couple slices of cantaloupe, and a slice of chocolate cake. It was good food and most senators are hearty eaters, even the female members.

The first few meetings I blinked to make sure this was really happening to me because I was in awe of these larger-than-life personalities. I was in high cotton, as we say in the South. Just a few months earlier I had been teaching my Emory University students about the courageous leadership Ernest "Fritz" Hollings had given South Carolina during the turbulent times of desegregation. Now I was sitting at the same table with this distinguished statesman. White-haired, tall, and erect as a ramrod at more than eighty years old, he looked exactly like a senator should. His low-country, Charleston accent is about as thick as my mountain twang, and sometimes his words are so sharp they can almost draw blood.

There was the great Robert Byrd, a man I had always felt an Appalachian kinship with, a man who pulled himself up by his own bootstraps out of the numbing poverty of the mountains of West Virginia. His album of old-time fiddle tunes has long been one of my prized possessions. No one makes more speeches on the Senate floor on a greater variety of subjects than this man who has served in the Senate forty-five years, longer than all but two people. His speeches are filled with Greek and Roman history, the Bible, Shakespeare, and long poems he can quote by heart. He makes speeches on all subjects imaginable—holidays, seasons of the year, family, dogs, and Senate history of which he has written four volumes.

Once when he was waxing eloquent on the virtues of spring-time, I asked a veteran senator standing nearby, "Where does he get all this stuff?" The longtime senator, who shall go nameless because he may want to get an appropriation out of Byrd's committee, joked, "He has fifty speech writers over at the Library of Congress—and they all are from West Virginia."

With his stem-winders against the president and the war in Iraq, this octogenarian has attracted a whole new generation of young people as fans. His website receives thousands of hits each day. I disagree with much of what he says, but I also recognize that I am serving with a legend.

Just as you can disagree with people with whom you feel kinship, the opposite is also true. I have little in common with Ted Kennedy, but ended up in 2002 cosponsoring a prescription drug bill with him and Bob Graham. History will judge this passionate man as one of the all-time great senators, and I respect immensely his work ethic and his tenacity. He also likes dogs, and that will pretty much endear anyone to me. He has a big black water spaniel named Splash that he used to take for a walk around the Hill until Splash took a code orange alert warning a little too seriously and bit a maintenance man working in the senator's office. After that, I didn't see Splash very much.

Diane Feinstein is as elegant and gracious in person as she is on television. Blanche Lincoln of Arkansas, the youngest woman ever to be elected to the U.S. Senate, I find to be independent, savvy, and gutsy. She gives me advice on Labrador dogs growing old, and I give her advice on sons growing up. Of course, I felt close to the former Democratic governors with whom I had served—Evan Bayh, Tom Carper, Ben Nelson.

But Lord, those current presidential candidates in my party! They are good, smart, and able folks, but if I decided to follow any one of them down their road, I'd have to keep my left turn signal blinking and burning brightly all the way. All left turns may work on the racetrack, but it is pulling our party in a dangerous direction. Whenever the candidates encounter a Political Action Committee group, they preen and flex their six-pack abs for "the Groups" like body builders in a Mr. Universe contest. Or, perhaps more appropriately I should compare them to streetwalkers in skimpy halters and hot pants plying their age-old trade for the fat wallets on "K" Street.

Just look at them. They are convinced most Americans will like what they see: John Edwards, shooting brightly through the skies like Halley's Comet. Joe Lieberman, steadily and surely plodding along, one labored step at a time, like Aesop's tortoise. John Kerry, the New Century's Abraham Lincoln, posing for *Vogue* in an electric blue wet suit with a surfboard tucked up under his arm like a rail just split. It made me wonder, are there more surfboards or shotguns in America? There's also Bob Graham, who made Florida a great governor, and Howard Dean of Vermont, with whom I served as lieutenant governor and governor. Clever and glib, but deep this Vermont pond is not.

I watched both Jimmy Carter and Bill Clinton up close in the early days of their campaigns, so I can recognize that familiar overdrive, that on-the-make-ambitious-to-be mind-set that all politicians have to varying degrees. With presidential hopefuls, it is multiplied many times over. They even come to have a certain kind of body odor that is all their own. Political groupies call it aura.

My best friend, former Congressman Ed Jenkins, had told me I would be impressed with Tom Daschle, with whom he had served in the House. I was, although the leader did seem a little puzzled when I told a reporter he was "as tough as a pine knot" and the reporter wrote "as tough as a pine nut." Back in Georgia an accurate quote of this old saying would have been considered a great compliment; in Washington it came out as if he were a condiment one could put on a salad. We have a lot of sayings in my neck of the woods that get the point across, even if they sometimes require an interpreter in Washington. If somebody is young and inexperienced, we say, "He's green as a gourd" or "He's not dry behind the ears." If a Georgia politician is upset, someone might say, "He is mad enough to chew splinters" or "He's all bent out of shape" or "He'll jump on them folks like a duck on a June bug."

Sworn in to the U.S. Senate by Senate President Pro Tem Strom Thurmond (R-SC).

There's even a saying I use to describe the Democratic whip, Senator Harry Reid of Nevada. Actually, it doesn't come from back home; it comes from Shakespeare, who had Lady Macbeth describe a "nice guy" with the phrase "the milk of human kindness." That's what I think about Senator Reid, who is as fine an individual as I've ever met in all my years in politics. Soft-spoken, thoughtful, always unfailingly polite, he's every senator's confidant—and the kind of person it just kills you to have to say "no" to, which is the great strength of his leadership.

In fact, they are all good people. They are decent, hard-working, and smart. They have been friendly and more than fair to me, even with my rough edges and strong opinions. Let that be underlined: Senate Democrats have been much nicer to me than I have either deserved or expected. But let this also be clear: I will not be bland in what I write, for I am not blind to what I see.

What I saw gradually drew back the curtain on Washington's political stage and over time my awe turned to shock, the Capitol's own version of shock and awe. I began to refer to the Tuesday meetings as the "TUMS-days" lunches as the ideology moved further and further to the left and the oratory was turned up to a decibel level that got so shrill for my old ears that I needed Tylenol to go along with my antacid. "The Groups" and money. Money and "the Groups." It was like a bad song you can't get out of your mind. I remember once we were urged over and over to attend a fundraising breakfast because a big labor union was going to give the party $20,000 for every senator in attendance. All fifty of us answering "present" could mean a million dollars for the party. Of course, I attended.

I began to think that the caucus, or at least the speakers who held forth at the lunches, sees the entire nation through the partisan prism of liberal states like California, New York, Maryland, and Massachusetts and believes that what is good Democratic politics there just has to be good Democratic politics from sea to shining sea. I naturally see the nation through the conservative prism of Georgia and the South, but I would never suggest that what was good Democratic politics in my neck of the woods would play well in Malibu and Manhattan.

I started to call this chapter "It's 'the Groups,' Stupid," because when "the Groups" say "frog," each party jumps. It really doesn't seem to matter how it affects the people or the nation as a whole. I'm sure this is true with both parties, but my yardstick says the Democrats clearly win the vertical leap when "frog" is yelled by AFSCME, the American Federation of State, County, and Municipal Employees with their 7.4 million members, and NARAL Pro-Choice America. To be fair, I'm sure the same could be said about the Republicans and their conservative groups like the NRA, the National Rifle Association.

The point I'm trying to make is if you are organized, have an acronym, an address inside the Beltway, and a PAC (Political Action

Committee), you are "in like Flynn." Just name your wish and one of the caucuses will bust a gut to romance you. On the other hand, if you are only an individual with some rural route address and don't have a PAC or even a PTPI (Pot To Pee In), then forget it, Bubba. If you're not part of an organized group with an office in Washington, the politicians won't even blow you a kiss, much less romance you.

Not long after I arrived in the Senate, I was sitting at my beautiful old mahogany desk in the Senate chamber, a desk by the way that has the names Russell, Talmadge, and Nunn carved in it. I was sitting there, probably frowning, when Senator Joe Biden of Delaware spotted me. He's been in the Senate thirty years, and he came over and sat down and said, "I've watched a lot of you former governors come up here and invariably you go through three phases (like a person grieving over a death, I suppose)."

"The first phase is disbelief. You just can't believe how legislation and decisions are made." He was right. I arrived in the Senate in the middle of the appropriations process and I could not believe the feeding frenzy.

"The next phase," he said, "is anger. You stay mad most of the time and you want to change the system and make it more orderly."

And then, finally, he said the third phase is "acceptance." I have not reached that third phase yet. Not even close. I'm still angry because of the petty partisanship on both sides of the aisle. Angry that one single senator representing less than one-fifth of 1 percent of the American people can stop any president of the United States—even during wartime—from making a crucial appointment to his own team.

I'm angry because of the thoughtless and needless waste of taxpayers' hard-earned money. Angry because soft money—big money—from special interests to both parties controls things in a way that is nothing short of bribery. Angry that this money pays for cynical consultants who sneeringly brag, "We do campaigns; we don't do government."

I'm angry at a process in which 59 votes out of 100 cannot pass a bill because 41 votes out of 100 can defeat it. Explain that to Joe Six Pack at the K-mart.

In recent years, the process has become so politicized and so polarized and so ingrained that we cannot even put it aside in time of war. It is a system that "Cuisinarts" individual thought into a mushy party pudding—a system that expects one to go along with the team even if the quarterback is calling the wrong signals.

One of these days, someone smarter and younger and more articulate than I is going to get through to the American people just how really messed up the federal government has become. And when that happens, the American people are going to rise up like that football crowd in Cleveland and run both teams off the field.

On the day Governor Roy Barnes appointed me to try to fill the big shoes left behind by our friend Paul Coverdell, I pledged to serve all Georgians and no single party. That is what I have tried my best to do, and that is what I will continue to do.

I took the first step in December 2000, when then president-elect Bush invited me and about fifteen others, including about five Democrats, to Austin to talk about his educational reform bill. I had already studied the Bush proposal and decided I was for it. I had watched what Bush had done for Texas schools when he and I were both governors. We both knew that improving education touches everything else. So I stood up at that small luncheon in Austin and told him that I, as a Democratic senator, would support his bill enthusiastically.

As I was leaving and he was thanking me for my statement of support, I told him, "Mr. President, I'm with you on a lot of things. I'm with you on your tax cut proposal." I saw in his eyes that my comment had registered. A couple of weeks later, I was in Texas Senator Phil Gramm's office. I had gravitated to Gramm early on. I had watched his speech on the Senate floor on CSPAN the day Senator Paul Coverdell had passed away so unexpectedly, and I wept with him as he said, "The heart of a lion beat in that frail body." I knew that to be true. I went to Gramm the first day I was in the Senate and told him how much I appreciated those remarks. We have a lot in common. We are both native Georgians. We're both graduates of the University of Georgia. We both worked as college professors. We both married way out of our league. We both love quail hunting. We both love a good dog. We've both had a yellow Lab named Gus. And we both had strong and caring mothers. That day we were talking about the Paul D. Coverdell Center at the University of Georgia—which is going to be magnificent—and Gramm mentioned that the president had told him of my comments about supporting the tax cut and asked would I like to join him in cosponsoring it in the Senate, I told him I would be honored. President Bush called me that night in my apartment and thanked me. That was in January. In May, Congress passed a $1.35 trillion tax cut. It is the largest tax cut since the one Ronald Reagan pushed through in 1981. Although I was the only Democrat supporting it for a long time, in the end twelve Democrats voted for it.

Unfortunately, the tax cut was compromised on its way to final passage. What started out as a broad, immediate, and permanent tax cut became one where some of the tax relief is delayed by several years. Then, to add insult to injury, the whole thing is set to be repealed in 2010. How can anyone make any long-range plans for a business or for a family with a here-today, maybe-gone-tomorrow tax cut, a tax policy that has a perishable date on it like a quart of milk? Of course it needs to be made permanent.

Perhaps it is because of my experience as a chief executive, but I went to Washington believing that a president—every president— should be able to select his own team and make out his own batting order. He is the leader and the one who ultimately should and will be held accountable.

My first test came with John Ashcroft, a man I know very well and had served with both as a governor and briefly as a U.S. senator. I was the first, and, for a while, the only Democrat publicly supporting his confirmation. In the end, when we finally got a vote, I was joined by seven other Democrats, and Ashcroft was confirmed 58-42.

A short time later, I broke with my party again and was the only Democrat to vote to confirm Ted Olsen as solicitor general. My vote made the difference, 51-49, and the president finally got his own man representing the government before the Supreme Court. I took that opportunity to tell my colleagues that "this never-ending, back-and-forth partisan ping-pong game of revenge needs to end—for the good of the country." I believe that strongly.

I also broke with my party on the ergonomics issue. By a very few votes, we overturned the outrageously expensive workplace safety regulations put in place by the Clinton administration at the last minute on his way out. Some estimates put the cost of the rules as high as $100 billion a year. There's a strong case that some changes should be made in workforce safety, and I will support some, but certainly nothing this extreme.

With all the support I was giving President Bush, it was only natural that some of the Senate Republican leadership would make an overture to me to switch parties or become an independent. As politely as I could, I expressed my long and active history as a Democratic office holder and how, with me, it didn't have anything to do with ideology; I was "born a Democrat."

This, of course, caused them to take a step back with a strange and puzzled look somewhat like the one the reader probably had upon reading that earlier chapter. No one can understand it except those older folks who live in Appalachia. When Senator Jim Jeffords of Vermont left the Republican Party in May 2001 and became an Independent, it turned the Senate upside down and gave the Democrats a one-vote majority. Again they came and the ante had gone up. I have no intention now or ever to disclose any details, but suffice it to say it was better than what Mr. Sterling got on the television program last year. For a freshman senator, it would have been, shall we say, "historic." Again, I politely declined, Tom Daschle became majority leader, and the rest is history.

I've always thought the most important decision any office holder makes is whom it is they really want to help. In that regard, in fall 2002, in the heat of a campaign season, the Democratic leadership laid on the straw that broke this old camel's back. It was the caucus position on homeland security. What came to be the main point of contention was whether any of the 170,000 employees of the new Department of Homeland Security could be moved around by the president in time of national emergency without all the hidebound restrictions of the Civil Service System complicating and delaying it. Every president before George W. Bush had that kind of authority, but because 2002 was an election year, the employee's labor union wanted to flex its muscle. They found a willing chairman in presidential candidate Joe Lieberman, whose Government Operations Committee had written the bill. The bill was driven by the American Federation of Government Employees and their cock-of-the-walk-president Bobby Harnage, who is always spoiling for a fight because, whether he wins it or not, the fight always helps to increase the 37.5 percent of government workers who are unionized. Their twin group, AFSCME, by the way, helped bring the state government of California to its knees. If allowed to continue unchecked and unchallenged, they will put the federal government in the same position.

In a floor speech on September 18, seven weeks before the general election and at a time when incumbent Georgia Senator Max Cleland led 54 to 33 percent in the polls, I told the Senate:

> Mr. President, Let no one forget that this debate on homeland security is being held in the shadows of the fallen towers of the World Trade Center. The smoldering fires may have gone out, the acrid smell may no longer burn our nostrils, the strains of "Amazing Grace" from the bagpipes may no longer fill the air, but,

make no mistake about it, the need to protect this country and prevent this from ever happening again is just as urgent.

So, how does the United States Senate meet this one of the greatest challenges of our time? I'll tell you. We talk and talk and talk. Then we pause to go out on the steps of the Capitol to sing "God Bless America" with our best profile to the camera. And then we come back inside and show our worst profile to the country . . . . We must give the president the flexibility to respond to terrorism on a moment's notice. He's got to be able to shift resources, including personnel, at the blink of an eye. So, why do we hold so dear a personnel system that was created in 1883 and is as outdated as an ox-cart on an expressway? I'll tell you why: because by keeping the status quo, there's votes to be had and soft money to be pocketed. That's the dirty little secret.

When the civil service was established well over a century ago, it had a worthy goal: to create a professional workforce that was free of political cronyism.

Back then, the solution was valid. But too often in government, we pass laws to fix the problems of the moment and then we keep those laws on the books for years and years without ever following up to see if they're still needed.

The truth of the matter is that a solution from the nineteenth century is posing a problem in the twenty-first. Especially when this country is threatened in such a different and sinister way.

Presently, we're operating under a system of governmental gout and personnel paralysis. Despite its name, our civil service system has nothing to do with civility. It offers little reward for good workers. It provides lots of cover for bad workers.

Hiring a new federal employee can take five months—*five months*. Firing a bad worker takes more than a year—if it's even allowable at all—because of the mountains of paperwork, hearings, and appeals.

A federal worker caught drunk on the job can't be fired for thirty days, and then he has the right to insist on endless appeals.

Productivity should be the name of the game. And we lose productivity when bad folks hold on to jobs forever or when jobs go unfilled for months.

It's no wonder there's resentment among our many good employees. I'd be resentful, too, if I watched bad workers kept on the payroll and given the same pay raises by managers who are intimidated by the complicated process of firing or even disciplining them . . . .

Now, I respect and thank the many good, hard-working federal employees. And I've tried to imagine myself in these workers' places at this particular time in history. I'm an old believer in that line by that wonderful Georgia songwriter, Joe South, "Before you abuse, criticize, or accuse, walk a mile in my shoes." But perhaps it's because I've worked for three dollars a day and was glad to have a job that I find their union bosses' refusal to budge for the greater good of this country so surprising. Union politics may be important, but it should never come before national security . . . . For the rest of our lives we will have to live with what we do on this issue. Will we choose to protect the special interests or will we choose to protect the lives of Americans?

Will we tie the hands of our president or give him the same unfettered flexibility other presidents have had before him?

Don't let this be one of those votes you'll look back on and ask yourselves for the rest of your lives, "What was I thinking of?"

The next day in a press conference, I tried again:

Of all the many things for my party to have a knock-down, drag-out fight over, the issue of national security is absolutely the worst. I can think of a no more unattractive picture our party could have projected six weeks out from an election. We are not doing our party any good by feeding the perception that Democrats are undermining the president of the United States on terrorism. And to Joe Six Pack in that Wal-Mart parking lot, that's exactly what we're doing.

I then brought my finger across my neck and said, "We're slitting our own throats." A week later I tried again, with one more plea.

> Have we lost our minds? Do you really want to face the voters with this position, this vote writ large on your forehead, like a scarlet letter?—and even larger on a 36-inch television ad two weeks before the election.
>
> The U.S. Senate's refusal to grant this president and future presidents the same power that four previous presidents have had will haunt the Democratic Party worse than Marley's ghost haunted Ebenezer Scrooge. It is unworthy of this great body not to even have an up or down vote on this bill. It is demeaning and ugly and over the top . . . . Frankly, I think it will be one of our sorriest chapters, certainly the worst in my short time here. A chapter where special interests so brazenly trumped national interests.

On election night, November 5, a ghost even scarier than Marley appeared in Georgia and in Missouri. As I had warned, this one did slit throats. Triple amputee and decorated Vietnam hero Max Cleland was defeated, dropping eight points in those few weeks— weeks that time and time again, eleven to be exact, the Senate Democratic leadership urged him to vote with those special interests. And in Missouri, Jean Carnahan, a fine senator and widow of my friend, Mel Carnahan, met the same fate. Don't just take the word of this bitter observer. Here's what Charlie Cook said in the *National Journal* on June 28, 2003:

> What would have happened if Senate Democratic leaders had decided during last year's debate on creating a Department of Homeland Security not to fight the GOP over the rights of the proposed department's workers? In the end, Republicans very effectively argued that Democrats were far more interested in trying to placate one of their party's entrenched interests, in that

case federal employees' unions, than in protecting the general public. Regardless of the merits of each side's arguments, most observers agree that Democrats came out of the fight looking bad, and that the party may have lost Georgian Max Cleland's Senate seat because if it. To be sure, many factors combined to turn the Peach State into a devastating political ground zero for Democrats last November. But the way the Democratic Party looked during the Homeland Security debate surely was one such factor. It's hard to argue that the decision by Senate Democratic leaders to focus on workers' rights was anything but a costly miscalculation.

Immediately after the election, the bill passed with the Democrats not saying the first word about protectionism for union and federal employees, which weeks before they had dwelled on. After the election the issue was not even mentioned. It had all been just politics by and for the Groups before the election. And, then and there, I decided I would never attend another Democratic caucus lunch on TUMS-days. I had seen and heard enough.

They were able and decent folks and they had been good to me, but, with the exception of only a handful, these Democrats went too far to the left for me.

I could not help remembering John F. Kennedy's prophetic warning years before about "party unity" and "what sins have been committed in its name." And then Kennedy's warning, "The Party which, in its drive for unity, discipline, and success ever decides to exclude new ideas, independent conduct, or insurgent members, is in danger."

"COMPROMISE": D.C.'S DIRTY WORD

7

Washington lawmakers have replaced dogs as best friends of "the Groups" and campaign consultants. The politicians are regularly petted and fed and they wag their tails and do tricks, the favorite ones being "Beg," "Lie down," "Stay," "Speak," and "Roll over." The special interest groups have to keep their pets obedient and performing in order to distort issues they must keep alive in perpetuity in order to make their jobs seem necessary. So, for these groups who make the decisions in our nation's capital, "compromise" is a dirty word. If one of their pets barks that word, they get their mouths washed out and put on a tighter leash.

Because of this, faith in politics as a decision-making process and government as the agent to carry out those decisions has hit an all-time low. The political climate of this nation is more hostile and partisan than at any time in recent history. I'm so glad these "issue idiots" weren't around back in the summer of 1787, when a group of political leaders met in Philadelphia's Independence Hall. They represented thirteen states—not only newly independent from

England, but also independent from each other. Most thought they were gathering to rewrite into a peacetime trade agreement the war treaty that had unified them against England. The idea of joining together into one nation under one central government was a radical shock to many of them, sprung on them by the leadership after they arrived. Debate raged throughout the summer. Some threw up their hands and left before it was over. Others hung around to see the final document, but then refused to sign it. In the end it contained only thirty-nine signatures of more than one hundred original delegates.

But the Constitution of the United States has proved to be one of the most remarkable documents the world has ever seen. Through the growth of thirteen little isolated colonies into a fifty-state, highly industrialized world power, its precepts have proven so fundamental, so true, that it has continued with only twenty-two changes through a Civil War, two World Wars, presidential assassinations, impeachments, and even one presidential resignation.

You see, what is so remarkable about the Constitution is not that it espouses a particular political ideology, but that it crafts a delicate balance among several ideologies that on the surface seem incompatible. Somehow, in the midst of the uproar and disgruntlement that surrounded its birth, the framers of the Constitution came to realize that democracy accommodates a healthy tension among several things—some of which today we would label liberal and others of which we would call conservative. Unlike today's representatives of the people, they also believed that a democracy requires a tolerance of opposition.

The central balance in the Constitution reflects the central struggle of its framing: the thirteen states wanted to maintain their independence on one hand, while gaining the benefits of community on the other. The compromise they finally reached on this issue permeates the entire document. Our nation has grown up around this delicate balance. As a people, we have a split personality—we glorify individual freedom while at the same time demanding

allegiance to community. Daily we mix both liberal and conservative ideologies in our practical political beliefs.

On the liberal side, we believe in helping those who have fallen
on hard times, in fostering equal opportunity and equal rights, in
providing broad access to housing, education, and health care. But
in pages right from conservative ideology, we also believe that traditional families do the best job of raising children, that hard work
and self-reliance should be encouraged and rewarded, and that
destructive behavior should be punished.

This mix of ideologies has worked because it is practical and
realistic. It recognizes that pure ideologies exist only in theory and
with special interest groups, whereas our daily lives are a constant
collision of various forces and beliefs that have to be reconciled.

In the real world outside the Beltway, most Americans are in the
middle. They mix both liberal and conservative ideologies in their
practical political beliefs. They believe in balancing welfare with
personal initiatives. They believe in balancing rights with obliga-
tions. They don't like either permissiveness or selfishness in their
extremes. They believe in a community obligation to provide
opportunity to individuals, who we then expect to take personal
initiative and make creative use of their resources to excel and
succeed.

And so we became a nation where even poor children had hope,
where if they worked hard and played by the rules, they could grow
up to be somebody. We were the land of opportunity. In this
context, we viewed politics as a useful process by which the
American people sorted out practical solutions for their problems.
Politics was the process by which we the people considered alternatives and agreed together upon solutions that were in our common
interests.

But the highly partisan and interest-group-driven politics in our
nation's Capitol leaves Americans disillusioned and disengaged.
They grow increasingly skeptical. When political debates are aired,
they change the channel. When polls open, they do not bother to

vote. The reason is that instead of using the political process as intended—to move toward the middle in reconciling the issues—American politics has been hijacked by shrill and well-financed special interests, where it is held hostage near the edges of the Groups' ideological extremes.

Some women's issues are examples of ideology on the edge. In everyday lives, most Americans are both feminists and traditionalists. In growing numbers, they represent two-career families. They know that working mothers are an economic necessity. We need them in our workforce, and they provide critical income to their families. Fully half of America's two-career families would slip below the poverty level if the mother quit her job and stayed home.

Working Americans love their families and want to do the best for their children. But they need two incomes to provide the good life. They want help in reconciling their jobs with their family responsibilities. The daily lives of real Americans have moved beyond the age of Ozzie and Harriet, but the political discussion remains stuck there. The debate could lead one to believe that women must either become hard-driven, uncaring professional machines or else stay out of the workplace completely. It is a polarizing Washington debate between two unrealistic extremes, and it contributes nothing to the solution of the problem.

The stay-at-home/working mother debate is just one of the important economic issues. Traditional conservatives say government is the problem and the corporate sector the solution. Traditional liberals contend that the corporate sector is the problem and government the solution. Well, Middle America sees the former as benefiting the rich and the latter as benefiting the poor. And they don't see anything in it for themselves either way. They don't want government to do everything for them, as die-hard liberals suppose. Nor do they want substantially less government, as die-hard conservatives espouse. What they want is common-sense government that works . . . for them.

Lack of common sense has resulted in political gridlock, and Americans are tired of it. They are sick of a process that is supposed to be in their interests, but is being carried on by the extremely well-financed and totally unforgiving special interest groups. They are frustrated because the issues on which political debate so often focus are not central to their daily lives. They want action on issues like the soaring costs of health care and college tuition.

Instead of polarized ideological debates over issues that often are on the fringe of most people's lives, we must make the political process a broadly based, practical discussion of reality. Americans want a government that focuses its energy on providing opportunities and resources as they work toward their dreams, toward making their lives and their communities better. They have lost patience with dysfunctional government.

We should remember, the Founding Fathers did not promise that government will provide happiness, but that Americans will have the opportunity to pursue it for themselves. In contrast, today's politics consists of different groups citing polls that tell people what is supposed to make them happy and calling that a substitute for opportunity. Regular Americans see through it all. The day has passed when you can piss on them and convince them it's raining.

This nation was not built by the dictates of highly organized special interest groups with their hundreds of millions of dollars in campaign contributions. It has been built by the personal initiative of individual Americans, working both separately and together with their neighbors in the communities where they live.

Today, our political process has a genuine disconnect with real live Americans. These Americans do not believe we are dealing with the issues that really concern them. They see absolutely no evidence of bipartisan efforts on their behalf. If they could see some, they would be willing to get involved again. They would recover the sense that they can control their destiny and that the system is responsive to them and works for them, rather than getting caught up in the never-ending partisan squabbling.

Aided and abetted by the special interest groups and political consultants who have their own axes to grind, must we always act like we're in a football game where there has to be a winner and a loser? We wouldn't even refer to politics as a game if there were *never* a loser—just a winner called "the People." The sorry answer is that the Groups and the consultants make their extravagant living off of promoting an issue and never accepting a result.

Myself, I'm a half-of-a-loaf kind of guy, and whether it's 75 percent or 65 percent or 50 percent—that's always better than 0 percent. You can eat half a loaf. Having no loaf at all may make a political point and save the issue for the campaign, but in the end somebody goes hungry—and I can tell you, it ain't the Groups or the consultants.

In Horace's *Odes,* written more than 2,000 years ago, there is some good advice about reaching an intelligent midpoint. He called it "the golden mean" and the quote goes like this: "Whoever cultivates the golden mean avoids both the poverty of a hovel and the envy of a palace."

Horace was wise. Our Founding Fathers were wise. Ben Franklin was perhaps the wisest of all and often would say, "Both sides must part with some of their demands." Democrat Harry Truman was wise when he got Republican Senator Arthur Vanderberg to author the Marshall Plan. Democrat Lyndon Johnson was wise when he got Republican Senator Everett Dirksen to help with the Civil Rights Bill.

John F. Kennedy, in his Pulitzer Prize-winning *Profiles in Courage,* put it so well in his opening chapter:

It is compromise that prevents each set of reformers—the wets and the drys, the one-worlders and the isolationists, the vivisectionists and the anti-vivisectionists—from crushing the group on the extreme opposite end of the political spectrum. The fanatics and extremists and even those conscientiously devoted to hard and fast principles are always disappointed at the failure of their government to rush to implement all of their principles and to denounce those of their opponents. But the legislator . . . alone knows that there are few if any issues where all the truth and all the right and all the angels are on one side.

Later he wrote, "Compromise need not mean cowardice. Indeed, it is frequently the compromisers and conciliators who are faced with the severest tests of political courage as they oppose the extremist views of their constituents."

Today's petty partisans would do well to remember that wisdom. Unfortunately for this nation, I believe the Groups and the consultants will continue to shout in their sycophant's ears, "Never compromise; it'll make a great issue in the upcoming election." Inside the Beltway, these tempting Sirens are every day luring the oh-so-vulnerable Odysseus onto the rocks.

41 Beats 59—
That Strange Senate Math

8

The United States Senate is the only place on the planet where 59 votes out of 100 cannot pass anything because 41 votes out of 100 can defeat it. Try explaining that at your local Rotary Club or to someone in the Wal-Mart parking lot or, for that matter, to the college freshman in Political Science 101. You can't, because this strange Senate math stands democracy on its head.

By name, this incongruous, obstructionist procedure is known as a filibuster. The word *filibuster* comes from a Spanish word for "pirate," and that is exactly what this procedure does. It hijacks the democratic process. Filibusters first caught the fancy of the nation after James Stewart, in Frank Capra's classic movie *Mr. Smith Goes to Washington*, made Mr. Smith a hero standing up to the Senate bosses on behalf of the people. But now, however, most Americans understand vaguely that in the Senate any member can stand up and talk endless drivel for hours in order to prevent legislation he or she opposes from coming to a vote. The process is so ridiculous that the filibuster, like that old comics-page blowhard Senator Claghorn,

has unfortunately become, in the minds of many, just another cari-
cature of the Senate, just another thing to laugh at, just more hot air
from the Cave of the Winds.

Realizing that with the scrutiny of television, the people would
not stand for such nonsense, the "Old Bulls" of the Senate fuzzed it
up. They made it subtler. These verbal gunslingers can now be
forced to shut up, and the process and the Senate move along
toward a vote if sixty members remove the cotton from their ears
and vote for cloture. A cloture shuts off what is called a debate but
isn't because it takes two sides talking to constitute a debate. If this
sounds confusing, it is meant to be. That is precisely the objective.

The short version of this debacle is that the way filibuster is
being used in the Senate gives the minority an absolute veto on just
about everything. In fact, the U.S. Senate has become similar to the
Security Council of the United Nations where one country can veto
the will of a clear majority and castrate the entire process.

Winston Churchill once said, "Democracy is based on reason
and fair play." Well, there's nothing reasonable or fair about what's
been happening in this august body. It's not just that it's an expensive waste of time and taxpayer money, but it's also a flagrant abuse
of majority rule, the principle that democracy operates on everywhere. Everywhere, that is, except in the U.S. Senate.

Rule XXII of the Senate is the reason for all this. It was adopted
in 1917 and was meant to move things along. President Woodrow
Wilson had lashed out at what he called a "little group of willful
men" who had blocked his proposal to arm our merchant ships
against German submarines. Sixteen senators could file a petition
against a bill or an amendment and if two-thirds approved it within
two days, debate was to be limited to one hour per member or one
hundred hours. Later it was modified to sixty votes, not two-thirds,
necessary to halt a filibuster. And in 2003, for the first time, it was
used to prevent a vote on the presidential judicial nominees.

The longest filibuster in congressional history was waged against
the Civil Rights Act in August 1957 by Senator Strom Thurmond of

South Carolina, when he held the floor for twenty-four hours and eighteen minutes. Wayne Morse of Oregon comes in a close second with twenty-two hours and twenty-six minutes. Probably the most entertaining was the Kingfish, Huey P. Long of Louisiana, who in 1935 only went on for fifteen hours, thirty minutes against one of President Roosevelt's New Deal proposals. When asked how he kept from answering the call of nature for that long he answered, "Why do you think I wore a navy blue suit?" Strom Thurmond had dehydrated himself in a sauna before taking the floor for his record-setter and didn't worry about that problem.

James Madison, the Father of the Constitution, feared some future political leaders would pervert the legislative process in just this way. He warned in Federalist Paper #58 that when it happened, "The Fundamental principle of free government would be reversed. It would be no longer the majority that would rule. The power would be transformed to the minority." I'm sure the man who wrote the Constitution is spinning in his grave.

Alexander Hamilton may be taking a couple of revolutions as well, because he agreed with Madison. He pointed out in his Federalist Paper #68 that the vice president was given a tie-breaking vote for "securing at all times the possibility of a definite resolution of that body." A "definite resolution"; how well put. But no one has said it better than Senator Henry Cabot Lodge in 1893, when obstructionism was not nearly as bad as it is today: "To vote without debating is perilous, but to debate and never vote is imbecile."

Years ago, when I was teaching freshman political science at Young Harris College, I always repeated the old story about the origin of the Senate. Thomas Jefferson was in France when the Constitutional Convention was being held. Later, he asked his friend George Washington, who presided over the convention, about the purpose of this upper chamber, the Senate. Washington, so the anecdote goes, then asked Jefferson, "Why do you pour coffee into your saucer?" "To cool it," Jefferson replied. Washington responded, "Even so, we pour legislation into the senatorial saucer to cool it."

Cool it, yes. But not freeze it into an ice cube. Truth is, there is nothing at all said in the Constitution about protecting Senate minorities. Our Founding Fathers, I believe, thought the smaller size, longer and staggered terms, as well as state legislation on the selection of senators, would provide more wisdom.

Some constitutional lawyers have argued that any kind of super-majority vote is unconstitutional, other than for the five areas specified in the Constitution: treaty ratification, impeachment, override of a presidential vote, constitutional amendments, and expelling a member of Congress. As I write this, Judicial Watch is doing just that. They have filed a lawsuit arguing that confirmation of judges is not specified in the Constitution and, hence, does not require a super majority.

That's one possible remedy. There are others. We could abolish Rule XXII that protects this travesty and let the U.S. Senate operate under rules like every other democratic legislative body in the world where a simple majority rules. That's about as likely as a day dawning in Washington without ten fund-raisers.

Or we could modify what I call the "two-track trick" or filibuster by stealth adopted a few years ago, where another piece of legislation is considered at the same time a filibuster goes its windy way. I call it "filibuster-lite." It's a way to avoid the inconvenience and pain of a real filibuster as if we are using powder-puff, 16-ounce gloves instead of bare knuckles. I'd much rather just duke it out in a real debate and get it over than try to deceive the public that no blood is being spilled. Many veterans of the Senate—not a newcomer like myself—have expressed dismay with the process. Henry Clay, generally recognized as one of our greatest senators, condemned the first organized filibuster when it occurred in 1837. Even back then, he thought there needed to be some workable limitation for endless debate. If only he could see what happened late in the twentieth century, Clay would be another grave-spinner. In the nineteenth century, there were twenty-three filibusters. In the last thirty years of the twentieth century, there were more than two hundred.

Two pieces of crucial legislation that filibusters have stymied over the years include the anti-lynching bill of the 1920s and abolishing the poll tax that was held up for twenty-two years from 1942–1964. The Civil Rights Act of 1964 was filibustered for ninety-three calendar days.

With Georgia's Senator Richard Russell as their leader and unlimited debate as their weapon of choice, a small band of Southern senators for years had managed to defeat or drastically weaken any civil rights legislation that came before the Senate. But it was different in 1964. The Senate membership had changed and President Johnson was pushing it with all his considerable power. He told the nation that passing the legislation would be the most fitting memorial that recently assassinated John F. Kennedy could be given. He also managed to peel off Minority Leader Everett Dirksen who often sided with Russell. In the end cloture was invoked 71-29 and the bill went on to pass by an overwhelming margin.

Obviously, both parties have used filibusters time and time again, one just as guilty as the other. In 1996, Democrats blocked a vote on a constitutional amendment on term limits and the Republicans blocked a vote to reform campaign finance. Many conservatives would disagree with me, but I happen to think the political process would have been improved if both those measures had passed. Certainly, it would have greatly weakened the current death-grip of the well-heeled special interest groups because electing their pet incumbents over and over with little or no opposition is what gives both the tremendous power they have. I call it "the dance," and it's nothing like that Garth Brooks song by the same name. After the music of election year stops, it's the public that gets screwed.

In the mid-1990s there was a bipartisan group of distinguished citizens called "Action, Not Gridlock" that came together with great ballyhoo, intent on reform and majority rule. Republican Barry Goldwater was among them. Then in 1995, Democratic Senators

Tom Harkin and Joe Lieberman introduced a rule change that I believe is the best that's been proposed.

Two years earlier, Harkin had let a committee hearing have it with both barrels: "There comes a time when tradition has to meet the realities of the modern age. The minority's rights must be protected. The majority should not be able to run roughshod over them, but neither should a vexatious minority be able to thwart the will of the majority and not even permit legislation to come up for a meaningful vote."

The Harkin-Lieberman plan called for a four-step process that kept sixty votes on the initial cloture vote, but decreased it by three votes with each of the next three cloture attempts until finally it got down to the majority of fifty-one. They argued, logically, that this would preserve the Senate tradition while giving the minority plenty of time to plead its case without blocking the majority forever. I liked this idea so well that in March 2003, I introduced an identical bill. In May I joined with Majority Leader Bill Frist in a modified version applying the process only to judicial nominees. That seems to have the best chance for any kind of change and I'm afraid that's not much. Both Harken and Lieberman now oppose what they so eloquently promoted a few years earlier.

As far as the fate of the Harkin-Lieberman rule change, the *New York Times* celebrated New Year's Day 1995 with a lengthy editorial beginning, "The U.S. Senate likes to call itself the world's greatest deliberative body. The greatest obstructive body is more like it." The article continued, "Once a rarely-used tactic reserved for issues on which senators held passionate convictions, the filibuster has become the tool of the sore loser, dooming any measure that cannot command the sixty required votes."

All of this came to naught, however, after the Republicans solidly opposed the amendment and Democratic Senator Robert Byrd who, like that mythical, hell-guarding, ferocious three-headed dog Cerberus, punctuated his opposition with the story of how Cato the Younger, in 60 BC, got the floor in the Roman Senate at

midday and valiantly spoke until sundown, the time of adjourn-
ment, in order to thwart one of Julius Caesar's proposals. That story
marked the end of the Harkin-Lieberman filibuster reform bill.
Never mind that Byrd didn't tell the rest of the story, that Caesar
was not thwarted and fourteen years later Cato committed suicide
while Caesar was at the height of his power and still going strong.

Now, I must admit I greatly admire and respect this man, Cato
the Younger. He was one of Rome's greatest statesmen, not at all like
his great grandfather Cato the Elder, who exemplified the corruption and hypocrisy that later undermined the traditions of
republican liberty. Cato the Younger was different. He was a moral
man and a great defender of the Constitution and the dominant
role of the Senate. That was his role and he always played it to the
hilt. His reputation was such that our Founding Fathers admired
him as a symbol of opposition to tyranny. In fact, George
Washington ordered a play about Cato performed to inspire his
soldiers at Valley Forge.

But, truth be told, Cato met an ignoble end. His reputation was
greater than his ability. After he was defeated by Caesar at the Battle
of Thapsus, rather than accept the generous offer of clemency from
his old antagonist, he committed suicide. And he botched that; he
didn't fall directly on his sword and it didn't kill him swiftly so he
tore out his own intestines with his bare hands. It gave "spilling your
guts" a new meaning and was a messy end for the First Filibusterer.
While today we can find many good books on Caesar, I have yet to
find one on Cato. So, you lovers of the filibuster, I say that is a
history lesson worth thinking about.

For all the good stories that have come down through the
centuries inspired by the filibuster, in the end, it has nothing to do
with ancient history.

The filibuster has nothing to do with the British Parliament.

The filibuster has nothing to do with coffee cooling in a saucer.

The filibuster has nothing to do with freedom of speech.

The filibuster has nothing to do with tradition.

The filibuster has nothing to do with the Constitution.

The filibuster has nothing to do with protecting minority rights.

The filibuster has everything to do with personal political power. It's about Alpha dogs defending their turf in that great big kennel under the dome.

"IF FINGERPRINTS SHOWED UP ON SKIN"

9

"If fingerprints showed up on skin, I wonder whose I'd find on you." That is a line from a Freddie Hart country music song that comes to mind when I think of politicians and money touching one another.

As you read this chapter, even as you turn to this page, political money is changing hands somewhere in Washington, D.C. It passes from the palms of those who have an ax to grind to someone in a position to help grind it. Although in the long run they get pretty heavy, the grindstones are carted almost daily to endless breakfasts, lunches, receptions, and dinners. The House and Senate schedules are not set to expedite the people's business or to solve the nation's problems. Each day "the schedule is set on the basis of when we have to be in recess so people can go to fund-raisers instead of working here to solve problems."

Those are not the words of this angry newcomer; they were spoken on the floor of the Senate on May 11, 1990, by David Boren, the highly intelligent and thoughtful senator from Oklahoma, who was also governor and today is president of the University of Oklahoma.

Never has that old saying about political contributions been so true: "He whose bread I eat, his song I sing." Listen closely and you can hear the harmonizing coming from those hallowed marble halls. *More money, more money.* It is the one song where both Democrats and Republicans know all the lyrics: *More money, more money. Of thee we sing.*

Because Washington feeds on greed, it breeds corruption. The result is the same shallow set of values that brought down the Roman Republic. If it continues unabated, it will bring down this one, too.

Now, truth to tell, I ain't exactly a virgin myself. When it comes to winning political races by raising millions of dollars and buying lots of television time, I've batted my eyelashes, flashed a come-on smile, and shacked up with the best of them. I did it three times in a row—once for the Senate and twice for governor—and it's the formula for success in politics today. But frankly, it's a rotten formula and the rules of this game need to change.

Perhaps I live in another world; I know I'm from another era. When I was elected to the state senate in 1960, I spent a little more than $400 in a competitive race in my mountain district. There were no disclosure laws, but I listed in the newspaper the few contributions I had and how I spent them. This year, state Senator Carol Jackson who represents that same district spent almost half a million dollars to be reelected.

When I ran statewide for lieutenant governor in 1974 with opposition in the primary, runoff and general election, I spent a total of $175,000. I used no television and no polls. I just got in a car and drove across Georgia. For more than a year, a friend and I criss-crossed the largest state east of the Mississippi, staying in cheap motels or in the homes of supporters. I'd go into a town, hit every office in the courthouse if there was one, visit city hall, visit the local businesses, drop by the local newspaper with hopes they'd take my picture. On the road, we'd search the sky for antennas, then follow them until we arrived at the local radio station. They'd always put me on for a few minutes and we'd usually talk about country music or sports. I kept up with both and could discuss them with great familiarity.

Even as late as 1989, after I decided to run for governor, I spent that year going to more than 250 individual fund-raisers, usually at $10 to $25 a head. Georgia has 159 counties. I visited them all.

That way of campaigning is as outdated as an eight-track tape. In my two races for governor and in 2000 when I ran for the Senate, I did it today's way. In the shadow of the majesty of the nation's Capitol, I locked myself in a room with an aide, a telephone, and a list of potential contributors. The aide would get the "mark" on the phone, then hand me a card with the spouse's name, the contributor's main interest, and a reminder to "appear chatty." I'd remind the agri-businessman that I was on the Agriculture Committee; I'd remind the banker that I was on the Banking Committee.

Then I'd make my plaintive plea for soft money—that armpit of fund-raising. I'd always mention some local project I had gotten or hoped to get for them. Most large contributors only understand two things: what you can do for them or what you can do to them. I always left that room feeling like a cheap prostitute who'd had a busy day.

I'd just douse myself with a little sweet-smelling political cologne called "rationalization" and take that money into another room, where high-priced consultants and pollsters would stick me in front of a camera and I would read the teleprompter for TV ads. Then, without even knocking, I would noisily intrude into strangers' living rooms over and over again via their televisions. And I would crawl in bed that night longing for the old days when I would have chatted with them in person at the local diner or civic club.

That is why as soon as I got to Washington I signed on as a cosponsor of the McCain-Feingold Campaign Finance Reform Bill and why I support drastic changes in the role money plays in politics today. It bans the raising of "soft money" by state and local parties on "federal-related activities," such as those ads that the Clinton administration used so effectively on Gingrich, Dole, and the Republicans in 1996.

The bill passed and is the law today. But, frankly, I don't think the bill goes far enough. Some say it's too strong; I think it's too weak. It's only a baby step in the right direction.

Over the past seven years, Congress has averaged 150 days a year in session. That means that there are 215 days we're not in session. Surely we could devote half our time to legislating and half our time to fund-raising. Fund-raisers should not be held on days Congress is in session. Spare the members the shame of voting on a bill the same day they get dollars from those who have an interest in that bill. Is that too much to require? Many states, including Georgia, have such a law presently. It didn't take long to realize why so many of these "events" are held in Washington. It's for the same reason Willie Sutton robbed banks: that is where the money is. Washington—in particular K Street, where the big lobbying groups have offices—is where the money is. And it's there for the asking; excuse me, for the begging.

Most Americans must surely wonder why we are reduced to begging. After all, those elected to Congress are paid $150,000 a year, which puts us in the top 5 percent tax bracket (that bracket the class warfare warriors call the "super rich"). In some cases, that's not enough to live on and so it seems spouses have to work as lobbyists. Now I have nothing against spouses working—mine has held jobs most of our fifty years of marriage. But as a lobbyist? Seeking to influence legislation? Give me a break. Talk about "gathering ye rosebuds while ye may." It gives a new meaning to "pillow talk." I cast no aspersions on the ones who do this, nor do I doubt their honesty. But in a business where "perception" is just about the same as "reality," it looks suspicious as hell. It looks like someone's riding the gravy train. It does not pass the smell test.

The big lobbyists of special interests have also found out that they can get more for their money by backing senators in small, less populated states where the money can go further. For one thing, the TV spots don't cost as much. Because of that, when special interests anoint the head of a small state candidate with dollar bills, his chances of getting his message across are dramatically increased. After all, the vote from a small state senator for your pet issue counts just as much as one from New York.

We should limit the inflow of money from out of state, either in the dollar amount or by percentage of total contributions. We should do away with or drastically limit all Political Action Committee money. Incidentally, 80 percent of PAC money goes to their "pet rock" incumbents. Once they get them there, they keep them happy.

During that debate in May 1990 on which I earlier quoted Senator Boren, he was interrupted by the venerable Robert F. Byrd, senator from West Virginia and historian of the Senate. Among other things he said these true and disturbing words: "We are kept busy with running around the country, holding out our hats and our tin cups." And then later as only Byrd can, he nailed it. "Do members vote their own mantra, their own hearts, their own consciences? That is a rhetorical question. Everyone in here knows that members do not vote their own minds and their own consciences on many issues, recognizing that the great body politic out there is not organized and represented, because we are so busy presenting the views of those who contribute to us in many instances, and voting against what we know in our heart is best."

During his more than four decades in the Senate, Byrd has put hundreds of thousands of words into the Congressional Record. None he has ever uttered have rung so true. He ended that statement, "So, the fault, Dear Brutus, is not in our stars, but in ourselves, that we are underlings of the special interests that contribute to our campaigns." "Underlings of the special interests." No one has ever said it better.

It is time to put duty before dollars, not only in Washington, but in our statehouses as well. The present system is rotten to the core.

"RETURN TO SENDER"

10

Before he got rich and famous and had daily columns in nearly four hundred newspapers, the late Lewis Grizzard and I used to go to Nashville at least once a year. We'd go to the Opry, see the sights, and hang out around the old Ryman Auditorium. Down the street a little from Tootsie's Orchid Lounge on Lower Broadway was a western-wear place called the Alamo. It was where all the stars bought their rhinestone suits and western-wear.

We went in there, killing time and looking around, and stayed about an hour. Lewis tried on a Stetson and a fringed suede coat that cost a thousand dollars. I tried on a pair of boots that cost fifteen hundred. When we were finally ready to leave, Lewis did not buy anything. I bought a pair of socks and a can of black shoe polish.

The cashier looked at us a little funny, like we were a pair of cheapskates. So I said to her, "You have got to understand, I'm in Georgia government and down there we look at what we'd like to have, then we buy what we can afford."

Lewis sent that story off to *Reader's Digest* and made $200. I never saw a cent. But the story makes my point. We should buy only what we can afford.

Washington, D.C. is the citadel of "champagne wishes and caviar dreams." Inside the Beltway, there is seldom any talk—much less, action—on cutting spending. Oh, it's often mentioned on the campaign trail, but amnesia strikes as soon as a candidate becomes an incumbent. And then, each year, as sure as the swallows return to Capistrano, every kind of federal program that the mind of man, woman, and the highly creative K Street groups can conceive ultimately finds its way into the budget. And, once there, it settles into a permanent home. Not for just a day, not for just a year, but always. Hey, that's a good line for a song. So is "return to sender"; that's exactly what we should do for the taxpayer.

There's no one on Capitol Hill or in this country who likes tax cuts more than I do. I've never seen one too big for me to swallow without water. Government takes too much from our taxpayers— big and little alike. Federal . . . state . . . local . . . taxes come at us from every direction. It's like a never-ending meteor shower.

Today, the American taxpayer works four months each year just to pay the government. We pay taxes from the cradle to the grave, and then when we're in the grave what we leave is taxed again. We pay taxes on everything, from hamburgers to Humvees. Five percent of the people pay 56 percent of the taxes. You're in that top 5 percent if your family income is more than $121,000 a year. Twenty-five percent of the people pay 84 percent of the taxes. If you make $53,000 a year or more, you are part of that 25 percent. Nearly 50 percent of the people pay 5 percent of the taxes. No, it's not even that much—it's 4.8 percent of the taxes.

This orgy of taxation is hurting the economy and damaging the American Dream. It hurts those folks running businesses who risk their capital to create jobs. It hurts investors—especially seniors— risking their money in a fragile stock market. And it hurts poor working families struggling to make ends meet. We need to leave more money in the hands of the American people so they have more to spend and to invest and to save and to expand their businesses. When that happens, the economy grows.

But, for Americans to be able to keep more of their money, the government must take less of it. That means lower taxes. It's the route President Kennedy took. It's the route President Reagan took. It's the route I took as governor three times. It's the route President Bush and Congress took in 2001 and again in 2003. It should be noted that the Kennedy tax cuts were put in place when the government was running a deficit and the debt was a larger share of the GDP than it is now. Relative to the size of the economy, the Kennedy tax cuts were three times larger than the first Bush tax cut and benefited the rich much more. Three of the Democratic Party's greatest heroes, Jefferson, Jackson, and Kennedy, were tax cutters. Judging by the presidential candidates for the election of 2004, you would never believe our party once had that tradition.

None of our presidential candidates voted for the Bush tax cuts and now, to varying degrees, they all want to do away with the cuts and finance various social programs. Dick Gephardt wants to repeal them all and do his massive health care initiative. Don't these candidates realize that during the coming campaign this position will translate that they want to raise taxes? That's the kiss of death. Walter Mondale in 1984 at least waited until the national convention to announce his tax increase proposal. These candidates can't wait that long. Even before the first votes are cast in Iowa and New Hampshire, they are, in the eyes of most voters, advocating the largest tax increase in history.

I happen to believe—and I think most Americans do also—that to let a tax cut expire after a designated period of time, or "sunset" to use legislative jargon, is the same as a tax increase. I promise that's how it will show up in negative campaign ads. So when it gets right down to it, few if any of the tax cuts will actually see the sun go down.

With tax cuts totaling some two trillion dollars in a period of less than three years as Bush has been able to do is truly significant. It is tax reform in every sense of the word, for its long-range effect will be to make the government revenue base not only smaller but also differently composed. For example, the capital gains and dividends rates are now the lowest since the Depression. If that isn't tax reform, then I've never seen it. I'm proud that I was a part of it as a principal cosponsor of both bills.

Politicians in both parties ought to remember why people don't like taxes in the first place. When I was a boy growing up in Young Harris, folks came to our house to pay their taxes because my mama was the city clerk and paying taxes was personal. I remember the questions and hearing them grumble each time they turned over their hard-earned dollars. What it taught me was that people don't complain about taxes because they are selfish or stingy. They complain because they simply don't believe they're getting their money's worth. Truth is, at practically every level of government, they aren't. That is especially true in Washington where lobbyists advocating more spending outnumber the ones who want less spending by more than one hundred to one.

Never forget that our forefathers opposed a system that put the power to tax in a faraway place like Washington. No one has ever spoken about taxes more eloquently than that great patriot Thomas Paine. "It is not the produce of riches only, but of hard earnings of labor and poverty. It is drawn even from the bitterness of want and misery." How's that from the author of *Common Sense*?

Thomas Jefferson, father and patron saint of the Democratic Party, as president had as his main goal the elimination of all taxes. When he was inaugurated for his second term he boasted that he had realized that goal: "Now it is the pleasure of every American to ask, what farmer, what mechanic, what laborer ever sees a tax gatherer of the United States?"

Nothing lasts forever, except those items that get into the federal budget. I see an awful lot of sacred cows grazing today in the lush green pastures of the federal government. Even though many of them quit giving milk a long time ago, we continue to feed them. Taxpayer dollars are the fodder sacred cows feed on because Congress forgets there is no such thing as "government money." Tax money belongs to the people who sent it.

I got into government in the belief that government can help people. But good government doesn't mean big government. Good government doesn't mean a generous government. Good government means providing basic services efficiently. Good government means not just asking how to make a program more efficient, but asking what would happen if we got rid of the program entirely. Government wastes time trying to make something more efficient when we don't need it in the first place. We are noted for our knack of inventing cures for which there is no known disease.

We now have the biggest, most expensive federal government in history. Why not start by abolishing vacant positions in every department except Defense and Homeland Security? Congress could set the example by cutting our own staff.

It's been said the Democrats blame the deficit on Republican tax cuts and the Republicans blame the deficits on the Democrats' social programs. As long as they can blame each other, they will never solve the problem. In 2003, some maintained that we couldn't afford tax cuts with a wartime economy, but they were the same ones who wanted more spending for entitlements.

I've been in politics for a long time and I thought I'd seen it all. But when I came to Washington in 2000, I was not prepared for the shock and awe of how matter-of-factly *both* parties in Congress spend huge amounts of money. Clearly, if we don't send overpayment of taxes back to those who paid them, politicians can always find a new way to spend the overpayment. That's why I don't want them to get their hands on this money to begin with.

It is so easy to dream up new programs, to dream unrealistic dreams. Willie Nelson has a great line in one of his songs: "Be careful of what you're dreaming, or your dreams will be dreaming you."

The fat in government is just like the fat in a package of ground beef. There are so many ways of cooking ground beef and each way is so delicious, you tend to overlook that it still has a lot of fat in it and may not be good for you when consumed as a regular part of your diet.

Most of us in Congress agree that we should try to run government as efficiently as a private business. How long would Sears or J. C. Penney survive if they overcharged you for a washer and dryer then told you they were going to keep your overpayment and spend it as they see fit? That's exactly what government does today at every level.

Critics of President Bush's tax cut used fancy charts and scare tactics to argue against giving the taxpayers their money back. They said we can't afford it, that it would erode Medicare and Social Security. They said the Bush tax cuts will put us in "the same mess" as Ronald Reagan's tax cut of the early 1980s, failing to mention that today's economic climate bears little resemblance to the one we faced twenty years ago. With stock prices down from their highs in 2000, we need our corporate balance sheets restructured now. Cutting the taxation on dividends will help do that.

Another way to prompt businesses to expand and invest is to cut the capital gains rate and I am pleased that the 2003 Bush tax cut did that, from 20 to 15 percent. We did not get into a slump just because consumer sales went down. Our economy withered because venture capital fell 74 percent. Capital spending by businesses was at its lowest in decades.

Throughout history, every time we have cut the capital gains rate, without exception tax revenues have risen, not fallen. The value of assets has always shot upward. Today, a capital gains tax cut should bring even better results because today's stock market is no longer the playground of the rich. Almost half of all Americans own stock. Almost one out of three who earns less than $30,000 a year

Talking tax cuts with Vice President Cheney and Senator Gramm.

owns stock. Come to think of it, aren't these the very people we Democrats say we want to help? The American middle class has become—for the first time in our history—the American investment class.

We should do away completely with the holding period for capital gains. Congress has experimented with many different holding periods over the years; it has been as long as ten years and as short as six months. Current law requires that an investment be held for more than a year before the investor qualifies for lower tax rates on his profits from the investment. Eliminating the distinctions between long- and short-term capital gains would make it easier on the taxpayer, and I think it would also raise productivity. A holding period of any length produces distortion. Eliminate the holding period and there would be an improvement in the liquidity and efficiency of the capital markets. The result: higher productivity, more output.

Talking tax cuts with President Bush and Senator Gramm.

Another reason for eliminating the holding period is that it would help simplify the tax laws. Among other things, tax shelters aimed at converting short-term gain into long-term gain would disappear. No need for them. The tax laws would be far simpler.

I believe that someday the income tax as we know it will be scrapped and a flat tax or some sort of consumption tax on goods and services will replace it. Either would simplify the tax code, though I lean toward the latter. It will be difficult to do. One reason is that there are tens of thousands of CPAs and tax lawyers who depend on its complexity for a living.

When the income tax amendment was ratified in 1913, the law was only sixteen pages. Today the tax code is close to 3,000 pages and the IRS tax regulations are more than 80,000 words. The cost to the American public to comply with this monstrosity is somewhere between $300 and $500 billion each year. It's mind-boggling to think what could be done with all that money, time, and effort. More than 135 million Americans will file a return each year and the IRS will have an argument with one third of them. That will mean more time, effort, and expense to all those taxpayers involved in that exercise.

If there were a consumption tax instead of an income tax, you would receive your full income and you would have more money to save. There would, of course, be no tax on savings, another good thing. There would be no "underground economy" where financial transactions are conducted with cash money by individuals and businesses "off the books" and never reported. Because of this taxpayers have to pay extra because of those who don't pay at all. With consumption tax, the more someone spends, the more they are taxed. The less someone spends, the less they are taxed. I believe that is fair. In fact, Congressman John Linder of Georgia has proposed this and, appropriately, calls it the "Fair Tax." Georgia Senator Saxby Chambliss and I have introduced it in the Senate.

Another thing that obviously isn't fair is this: when our seniors contributed to Social Security through the payment of payroll taxes, they did so with the understanding that later in time of need they would receive those benefits tax-free. But starting in 1993 these benefits were taxed. This is wrong. Every penny counts with most of these people and this is the government taking money away from them when they need it for food, heating, and health care. We should repeal this tax. The legislation I cosponsored with Senator Richard Shelby (R-Alabama) would phase out this tax until it is completely eliminated.

One of the most interesting proposals I've come across is the Alternative Maximum Tax or "Max Tax," as it is called, with a flat rate of 25 percent of all gross income. That would certainly simplify things, but I always remember what Milton Friedman once said about a contest between the special interests of Washington against the rest of America: "Washington always prevails."

ABORTION AND A GOD ABOVE

11

Bill Clinton, Jesse Jackson, Al Gore, and Dick Gephardt, to name a few, started their political careers opposing abortion. Over the years they all changed their positions to pro-choice. My own evolution on this issue has been just the opposite. Personal experiences again reshaped my thinking.

My mother was a pioneer, breaking down barriers for women long before feminism was a word, before there was a NOW or before there was any discussion of an Equal Rights Amendment. In the late 1940s she was one of only two female mayors in all of Georgia. Earlier she was the first woman to serve on a jury in our county and for years was the only woman on the town council. Physically strong as an ox, she also painted delicate watercolors. She nearly always won the blue ribbon for her flower arrangements at the local mountain fair. She was as tender with little ones as anyone I've ever seen and they adored her, but she could be as blunt as the blow of a sledgehammer with men who disagreed with her. If you wanted to know her opinion, you would just have to ask her and she would give it to you with the bark still on. Sometimes you didn't have to ask. When one of the local preachers grew whiskers, she told him, "You need to shave that beard off."

As I have said, when the women's movement came along in the 1960s and 1970s and I was asked what I thought of women's rights or women being involved in politics, I could honestly reply, "I never knew anything else." With such a strong female for a mother and a similarly strong wife (she once was one of two female bank presidents in Georgia), I have always accepted strong, opinionated women as a fact of my life. I never questioned their ability, their judgment, or their equality. I certainly never felt superior to them because I happened to be a man.

So, there was a time, when the question of abortion came up, I automatically answered that a woman should make that decision about her body. Without a shred of soul-searching, I supported the *Roe v. Wade* decision by the Supreme Court. I said, "Leave it to the woman, her God, and her doctor."

But, over time, I came to realize this is a much more complicated issue than that. Even from my first political stance on abortion, I qualified wholehearted support based on how the law should be applied to minors. I took the position that parents should be notified and consent obtained before a minor could proceed.

Also, I took the position that public funds should not be used for the procedure. About the same time I modified my stance again, viewing abortion as appropriate only in the first trimester. Then as governor, I signed a state law in 1997 outlawing the terrible procedure of partial birth abortion. Still, I stuck with my position of supporting abortion, but with all these qualifications. I was personally comfortable with those positions. Further, polls showed the majority of the American public was in favor of abortion, but with some qualifications.

I can accurately date the genesis of my evolving beliefs on abortion back nine years to when my great-grandchildren began to arrive. I began to seriously wrestle with where I was on the real question. I began to pray earnestly for God's guidance. Shirley and I were married young and had children early. So did my oldest son. But then when our grandchildren began to have children at an early age, we worried and wondered how they would make it.

But fast-forward a few years. At Christmastime around the hearth in the living room in Young Harris, four great-grandchildren gather with the rest of our big family. Like past generations, they're excited and anxious to open their presents. Their parents counsel them to wait, as they had to wait when they were children, and I thank God the circle is unbroken. I look at nine-year-old Jacob, who loves to read to his six-year-old brother, Joshua, and three-year-old sister, Mary. I see Jasmine, now a year old, and I give thanks for these precious little human beings. Even though their young parents struggle tremendously to take care of them, I know how richly blessed we are that they were not four of the 42 million who have been aborted over the past thirty years, that they are alive, a fifth generation to celebrate Christmas in that old house.

I believe the thinking of many Americans is changing on this subject. New science and technology can now show the heart of the unborn baby beating in the mother's womb. I saw it on the front page of *Newsweek*, no less. I remember my grandson, only twenty, carrying a sonogram around to show off his yet unborn, but so alive daughter. It gave new meaning to the old Roberta Flack song "The First Time Ever I Saw Your Face."

I know it is wrong to take these lives. For me it is no longer a political issue but a moral one, as it should have been from the beginning. I hope someday *Roe v. Wade* will be reversed. I will support justices to the Supreme Court who I think will do that, but I will not use this issue as a litmus test. I have come to believe that when some rail about having that "choice," they really are saying the woman should have that "comfort." The most poignant sight for me at this year's annual pro-life march and demonstration in Washington, D.C., was the large number of women holding signs saying they regretted their abortions.

One of the things I've never been able to reconcile is that most of the pro-choice advocates are at the same time anti-death penalty advocates. It seems strange they shed tears for someone who has been found guilty of having committed heinous crimes, but cannot find equal compassion for an innocent infant who has hurt no one.

Talk show host Sean Hannity has made a point that also hit home with this old history teacher. It had vaguely crossed my mind but Sean wrote about it eloquently in his book, *Let Freedom Ring*. He reminded us of the similarities between *Roe v. Wade* and the Dred Scott Decision in 1857, the latter of which ruled that slaves were property and denying that property to a slave owner was unconstitutional. In 1972 *Roe v. Wade* maintained that abortion is a private right and that denying that right to women was unconstitutional. He went on to point out that "The Constitution stands for neither slavery nor abortion and yet in order to reach their conclusions, the justices in both cases had to treat human life as if it were something else."

The comparison of abortion with slavery does not stop there. The elite, arrogant plantation owner believed his own self-interest to be more important than the slaves' self-interest. A woman who favors abortion believes her self-interest comes before the unborn's self-interest. In each case, the judgment is a moral one, made deliberately. What could be more arrogant than to believe one has the right to designate a life not worth living?

Lincoln opposed slavery; he thought it was immoral and argued that "a house divided against itself cannot stand." When he met Harriet Beecher Stowe, he remarked this was "the little woman who started the war," meaning she was the person who put a human face on the horrors of slavery with her book *Uncle Tom's Cabin*. In a similar way, that cover of *Newsweek* with the photograph of a sonogram showing so clearly that little human being in its mother's womb has helped put a face on the unborn. Just as Dred Scott was overturned, I believe *Roe v. Wade* someday will also be rejected.

One of the most encouraging signs I've seen of this is the growing percentage of teenagers and college-aged Americans who are more conservative about abortion rights than those of a generation ago. When I returned to the college classroom in 1999 after a fifteen-year absence, I was surprised by this. Many were outspoken against abortion. I didn't bring the subject up in class, but one day two female freshmen stayed behind to ask my position on abortion. My thoughts were still evolving and I may have stammered as I listed the qualifications I believed should be placed on the procedure. They would have none of that "gray" reasoning; it was black or white with both of them. It was solely and completely about the life of the baby and nothing else.

I believe this is a national trend. Support for abortion rights has steadily dropped for a decade, from 67 percent in the early 1990s to 54 percent in 2003. A *New York Times*/CBS News poll found that "among people 18 to 29, the share of whom agree that abortion should be generally available to those who want it" was only 39 percent, down from 48 percent in 1993.

Some maintain this shift is occurring because a ten-year decline in teenage pregnancy has reduced the demand for abortion. Some credit the abstinence program in many schools. Others say the stigma of giving up a child for adoption is not as great, thus there are more adoptions. All of these play a part, but I think the reason this is happening is that the debate has shifted from the right of the woman to the right of the baby. Note I did not say "fetus." I was appalled when in the Laci Peterson murder case a National Organization for Women (NOW) proponent objected to calling it a double murder because it wasn't possible to determine whether the little body that washed ashore was "born" or "unborn." Twenty-six states have fetal homicide statutes and I am a cosponsor of such a bill in Congress. Ultrasound technology has proved the unborn baby is human, and abortion has become the moral and ethical issue my mother—that strong woman—always maintained it was.

"BY THE SWEAT OF ONE'S BROW"

12

Too many politicians just don't understand that most people with any pride or self-esteem do not want something for nothing because it belittles them.

I still remember how that point was driven home to me. Back when school attendance was made compulsory in Georgia, the truant officer—or visiting teacher as she was known in my county—was a woman named Mrs. Mary Will Phillips. She combined tough love and a gentle spirit to influence parents who saw little benefit in sending their children to school. There was one family that felt they couldn't provide for their children clothes their classmates wouldn't look down on. So when Mrs. Phillips found that out, she gathered up some donated clothes and took them to that family. Still, the children did not appear in school. She went again to the home. As she got on the porch she saw some hound dogs lying in a bed made from the clothes she had given the family a couple of weeks before.

Most people would have been angry, but she understood mountain pride. She said nothing about the dog bed. Instead, she told the mother she had some work for her and she would pay her with some clothes for the children. The mother gladly accepted. She came to Mrs. Phillips's house and worked for the children's used clothes. I tell my political friends this story when they want to lavish gifts on needy but prideful people.

Over and over, when I was growing up, my mother would say, "Take what you want, sayeth the Lord, take it and pay for it." I was a grown man before I realized that's not in the Bible. It was my mother's scripture and what she meant was that one could have anything they want in life, but they have to pay for it. Everything has a price. If you want to be a great athlete or musician, you pay the price of practice. If you want to go to college, you have to pay the price of studying and making good grades.

There is a story about Gary Player, the great golfer, who once had a person come up and gush, "I'd give anything if I could hit a golf ball like you." Player stopped and looked his fan square in the eye. "No, you wouldn't. You know what it takes to hit a golf ball like I do. I'd go out every day and hit a thousand balls. My hands would bleed and I'd go hold them under cold water and then I'd go out and hit another thousand. That's what it takes to hit a golf ball like I do." He was saying what my mother had always told me. "Take what you want. Take it and pay for it."

That should be the philosophy of any government program, too. But it's just one of many things government doesn't understand. Here are some others:

As powerful as government is, it can only do so much by itself. Government can never take the place of parents in raising children. Government can never take the place of families and churches and synagogues in teaching values. Government can never take the place of people in our communities working together and looking out for each other.

Government can, of course, provide opportunities and encouragement. Government can help the next generation become better off. But government cannot make the next generation better. Government can set goals. But only people can touch souls.

No one has to do a briefing paper on poverty for me. I knew it firsthand and up close. However, I also saw firsthand the determination and hard work with which my mother supported her family. She lived that passage in Genesis—"By the sweat of thy brow shall thy eat food."

When I became governor, I crafted a program of welfare assistance that was inspired by that same passage. It was a program simultaneously providing opportunity and requiring responsibility. It put Georgia on the leading edge of welfare reform around the nation and eventually led to reform on the federal level.

My goal was to break the cycle of dependence on public assistance by enforcing parental responsibility and helping families become independent. Key elements of the changes in welfare policy included a cap on benefits to any mother having another child while on assistance, a teenage mother's residency requirement, and employment incentives.

The family cap became the more controversial aspect of the plan. Under it, a parent who had received welfare benefits for twenty-four months received no additional cash assistance if she had a child while on welfare. Medicaid coverage was provided for the additional innocent child or children, but the mother herself got no additional benefits.

I also believed, and still do, that a key step in helping unmarried teenagers avoid welfare dependency is to require young mothers to live in their parents' home where they can receive the help and guidance they need to become effective parents themselves. So, most unmarried teenage mothers had to live with a parent, legal guardian, or other adult relative or in a supportive living program supervised by an adult. Exemptions were allowed only if needed to protect the mother and child from abusive living situations.

You would have thought I was Satan straight from hell. A headline in the *Atlanta Constitution* blared "Miller's Welfare Plan Punishes Kids in Poverty." The director of the Georgia Citizens Coalition on Hunger declared, "We want to see the governor's package killed." The local lobbyist for NOW criticized the proposals as "grossly misjudged and potentially dangerous." The fight over the bill lasted the entire session and it was not approved until in the closing hours of the last night of the session.

Then it was up to an African-American Democrat named Michael Thurmond to make it work. He did a superb job and has subsequently been elected twice as Georgia's commissioner of labor. Under his guidance, the state welfare rolls dropped to their lowest levels in a quarter of a century. This unprecedented decrease in caseload was especially significant considering Georgia's remarkable population growth from 5.4 to 8.3 million over the last two decades.

I felt a strong message concerning personal responsibility needed to be sent to people who had additional children while on welfare.

The program did not tolerate those who were able but unwilling to work. Able-bodied welfare recipients with no children under age fourteen, who quit or refused to take a suitable full-time job paying at least minimum wage, had their cash benefits reduced, while the children continued to receive assistance. We made exceptions for those who took care of ill or disabled household members, those who were in school or in job training programs full-time, and those who could find no transportation to their job.

The job training and education program we developed to prepare welfare recipients for work was called PEACH or Positive Employment and Community Help. We expanded PEACH to all 159 counties and later changed its name to WorkFirst.

I directed the Department of Human Resources to offer opportunity and incentives for people to take responsibility for their own lives, to encourage them not to surrender to a faceless bureaucracy, where the check just shows up automatically in the mailbox each month. Finding a job became the number-one goal for every person who walked into an office intending to apply for welfare, food stamps, or Medicaid. Waiting rooms in these county welfare offices were turned into job search centers and childcare facilities.

Through more personal involvement in daily lives, I wanted to stop the decades-old practice of simply putting checks in the mail, month after month, year after year, in some cases generation after generation. Cash assistance in Georgia was limited to a total of four years. We focused on helping people get the skills for the jobs they needed. We emphasized pregnancy prevention, especially among teenagers. So, when the federal Personal Responsibility and Work Opportunity Act was finally passed in 1996 after much national debate, Georgia was in an excellent position to implement federal reform.

Georgia's WorkFirst program evolved into the federal Temporary Assistance for Needy Families (TANF) program beginning in 1997. After vetoing two welfare reform bills not to his liking, President Clinton finally signed one in the election year 1996, keeping his promise made years earlier of "changing welfare as we know it."

With the implementation of TANF, welfare was no longer considered an entitlement but a program that provided temporary cash assistance while moving people into employment. It allowed states wide latitude to design programs to meet their own needs and to establish rules even more stringent than federal requirements. For example, federal rules limited welfare recipients to sixty months of assistance over a person's lifetime. Georgia's rules limited assistance to forty-eight months. At the time, I said, "Our plan strikes a proper balance between fairness and toughness. The citizens of Georgia are willing to help those who want to help themselves, but they will not tolerate those who refuse to work and those who are unwilling to obey the law or accept their parental responsibilities."

The program also required teen mothers receiving assistance to stay in school, adult recipients to ensure their minor children attended school, and parents to participate in parent-teacher conferences.

Family cap provisions already in place were also strengthened.

The percent of families participating in work activities and the number of hours they had to work per week rose each year. By 2002 at least 50 percent of adults or care givers had to work at least thirty hours per week. Georgia was one of a handful of states that would not allow minors with children of their own to live outside their parent's home if they received TANF. This allowed children to receive the help they needed to be more effective parents and increased the possibility of them graduating from high school.

People who failed to cooperate in establishing paternity or obtaining child support were denied assistance or had their benefits terminated. In addition, those found guilty of drug felonies or serious violent crimes had their assistance terminated forever. For failure to comply with mandatory work requirements, our "Two Strikes" policy mandated a 25 percent reduction in benefits for the first offense and termination of assistance for the second. To ensure fairness and consistency in potential sanctions, we agreed to the creation of a board composed of local public officials and private citizens to review decisions to terminate welfare benefits.

There is no doubt in my mind that a lack of affordable childcare contributes to welfare dependency. In fact, in a society with an increasing number of single-parent households, lack of childcare may be the single greatest obstacle hindering efforts to escape welfare. Georgia significantly increased childcare resources available to welfare recipients who are receiving training to enter the work-force. Childcare is also available to employed persons who recently left the welfare rolls, increasing the likelihood they will maintain successful employment. In addition, childcare is available to low-income families who are at risk of going on welfare.

One of the reasons TANF passed in 1996 was the provision that it would have to be reauthorized in 2002. Unfortunately, the bill got bogged down in that year of gridlock and was postponed. Many of my Democratic colleagues saw this was a chance to make changes that I believe would weaken it.

I favored reauthorization and the changes President Bush recommended. Even though at the end of fiscal year 2002 caseloads had been reduced by 59.2 percent since 1996, he proposed keeping the same level of funding at $17 billion. That represents an expenditure of $16,000 per family. He makes the point that if $7,000 per family was good enough in 1996, more than twice that amount should be adequate now. I agree. Child poverty has fallen sharply. Among African-American children under age three, the most vulnerable, it had decreased to 35 percent in 2000 from 57 percent in 1992. Of course, that is still far too high and, along with Hispanic children, is three times that of whites. But the program is working and millions have had their lives changed in a positive way. The program has been a success anyway you want to measure it. Why would anyone want to slow this kind of progress?

President Bush has suggested that every state should be required to have 70 percent of the people on welfare today working a forty-hour week within five years. Senator Ted Kennedy and a number of other liberal Democrats say that is too tough a requirement. I don't think so. You see, the word "work" is given a broad interpretation in the president's proposal. It can mean on a job, or in school, or on job training, or even in alcohol or drug treatment programs. That seems more than reasonable to me. President Bush also speaks of strong marriage as a national goal. Who can disagree with that?

Some may call the Bush bill a tough approach; I call it a hopeful approach. It seems to me that we are saying to those on welfare, we have faith you can do it. You can work and be self-sufficient. We are going to help you do that. We are going to grant you that opportunity. We're going to smooth the path from welfare to work. But we are going to insist that you become like the woman in Proverbs who "rises while it is not yet light, works and eats not the bread of idleness."

GROWING UP WITH GUNS

13

My uncle Hoyle Bryson was a legendary athlete in our little valley. Right after he married my Aunt Euzelia, they went away for him to play professional baseball in faraway, exciting-sounding places like Tallahassee, Florida; Tarboro, North Carolina; and Portsmouth, Virginia. He was a pitcher with a blazing fastball and great control. In those days there was no such thing as a "relief pitcher" and his manager used him so much his arm "just went dead." Hoyle and Euzelia came back home and built a little house next door where they raised my two cousins, Bob and Bryan. He went to work for the local REA as a lineman climbing poles and stringing wire as electricity came to our homes for the first time from the newly formed TVA lake a few miles away.

Descended from one of the original settlers in the valley, Hoyle was a true mountain man and a crack shot. He also trapped wild animals and sold their hides to support the family. A possum hide would bring fifty cents, a muskrat or a skunk two dollars. He could live in the mountains, forests, and caves for days at a time. He hunted for food and for fun. Every Friday night, for well over half a century and still today as he nears ninety years of age, he has taken his hounds out into the woods to hunt fox.

Getting to go raccoon or opossum hunting with Uncle Hoyle was a great treat on winter nights. We'd take an oil lantern and "Coley," a beautiful black and tan hound, and prowl the woods until Coley would "strike a trail" and begin barking in the certain way all coon hunters recognize and love. After a few minutes, he would start barking a different "treed" sound and we'd race stumbling through the woods until we found the dog with its front paws up on the side of the tree, yapping like crazy.

Hoyle would shine his three-cell flashlight up in the tree. Two shining eyes would glare down from high above and we boys would exclaim, "It's a big 'un." Along with our little .22 caliber rifle, we boys carried an ax. If the trees weren't too tall, we'd cut them down. If they were easy to climb, we would shinny up and shake out the raccoon, or if the raccoon were in a very tall tree, Hoyle would shoot it out. Whatever method, when the animal hit the ground, Coley would be all over it until Hoyle pulled him off and put the critter out of its misery with a sharp blow with the back side of his ax or just stomped its head. To those who have never been hunters, it sounds cruel by today's standards, but we didn't give it a second thought, if we thought about it at all. We were hunting to eat and sell its hide, and we put the creature out of its misery as quickly as possible.

Uncle Hoyle had a beautiful Winchester 16-gauge pump shotgun. I can see it now. It was cradled on two big nails driven into the wall of his house next door in Young Harris. It was magnificent. Sometimes, I'd take my shoes off, stand up on the couch, and reach up and touch it.

Hoyle fed his family and me with that gun. He'd go off early on foggy fall mornings up in Kirby Cove where tall Hickory trees grew and beginning in late August squirrels could be heard dozens of yards away as they "cut" the hulls off hickory nuts.

Hoyle had an old hunting coat made out of canvas with slits cut on each side where he could store his prey in the baggy back. My cousins and I would wait to greet him when he returned, excited to see what he had brought home. He'd reach through the slit and bring out a squirrel, then another and then another. We'd ooh and aah as we'd sometimes count seven or eight squirrels. He had a little trick. When we thought he'd brought them all out, he'd act like he didn't know it and with a big grin reach back and get the last one. Then we'd watch him take out his pocketknife, give it a few swipes on a whet rock to sharpen it, and then he'd skin and clean his kill. Later we would have delicious squirrel and dumplings for supper or fried squirrel for breakfast.

I recount these childhood stories about Uncle Hoyle because they bring back wonderful memories of how I grew up and they remind me how guns have always been a part of my culture.

I got my first shotgun, a 20-gauge Stevens single-shot, when I was fourteen years old. Then I did what Hoyle did and his father before had done, I went hunting. Now my fourteen-year-old grandson hunts squirrels in those same mountains with a shotgun.

I grew up with a cousin named Eric England, who is about my age. He joined the Marine Corps before he finished high school and I followed him three years later. Eric made the Marines a career and served as a sniper in Vietnam. He was on the Corps' elite rifle team for many years. He set a record in long-distance shooting in 1968 that has never been broken. The rifle he used, a Winchester Model 70 bolt-action 30.06, is in the NRA museum in Washington, D.C. I'm sure that a love of guns is one thing that keeps these two old cousins as close as we were as teenagers.

So, when I was making the keynote speech at the National Rifle Association banquet in April 2002 and remarked that I had more guns than I needed but not as many as I wanted, it was more than just a wisecrack. I do own a bunch.

When I was running for reelection as governor in 1994, some of my advisors urged me to change my long-time position on guns and the Second Amendment. They said the polls showed that most Georgians favored gun control. But I know Georgia and my gut instinct told me their polls were wrong. I said, "I think you're asking the question the wrong way. Ask whether they agree or disagree with this statement: 'Whenever I hear politicians talking about gun control, it makes me wonder if they understand my values or my way of life.'" You know how many agreed? 73 percent!

Too many people don't understand that the gun issue is not just about guns. It's about values; it's about personal freedom; it's about individual responsibility. When we trust a candidate with our vote, we trust them to serve our values.

Our values say we have to protect our freedom by all means possible and guns are one of those means. That's why I was a cosponsor of the legislation allowing pilots to carry a firearm in the cockpit. I asked the Senate, "Will someone please explain to me the logic that says we can trust someone with a Boeing 747 but not a Glock .9 millimeter?" No one could, and it was finally included in the Homeland Security Act.

A firearm might have allowed our pilots to stop those terrorists from taking over four of our airplanes and killing thousands of Americans on September 11, 2001. A stun gun would never have done the job—not on September 11 or any other day. When a pilot has only one chance to stop a terrorist—when he is the last thing standing between landing the plane safely or having it shot down by a missile from a U.S. fighter jet—that pilot needs to be armed with a gun.

When I was governor in Georgia I started an "instant online background check" on people buying rifles, shotguns, and handguns. A terminal is installed at each firearms dealer's place of business and is operational seven days a week from 8:00 A.M. to 10:00 P.M. Since it was set up, more than 1.2 million background checks have been made and 63,000 sales have been denied. Under Georgia law, it is a felony for any person who has been convicted of a forceful felony to even attempt to purchase a firearm. It has worked well and no law-abiding citizen's Second Amendment rights have been violated.

A couple of years ago, an Emory University professor named Michael E. Bellesiles wrote the most distorted view ever published about the role of firearms in early America. It was called "Arming America." It delighted anti-gun reviewers by claiming that colonial militias were ineffective, that settlers seldom engaged in hunting, and that colonists had little interest in owning firearms. The *New York Times* gave it a glowing, almost giddy review of several pages, as did other liberal media.

In Bellesiles's America-in-Wonderland, colonists were a bunch of naive, wishy-washy peaceniks. Well, tell that to the British Redcoats who tried to cross Concord Bridge! Tell that to Thomas Jefferson who said, "No free man shall ever be debarred the use of arms," or Samuel Adams who said, "The Constitution shall never be construed to authorize Congress . . . to prevent the people of the United States, who are peaceable citizens, from keeping their own arms."

Tell that to James Madison, the Father of the Constitution, who explained that the document preserves "the advantage of being armed which Americans possess over the people of almost every other nation where the governments are afraid to trust the people." Tell it to Thomas Paine, the writer of *Common Sense*, the pamphlet that inspired the Revolution. He wrote, "Arms discourage and keep the invader and plunderer in awe, and preserve order in the world." Finally, consider the patriot Patrick Henry, who warned us to "Guard with jealous attention the public liberty. Suspect everyone who approaches that jewel."

Well, I "suspect" Professor Bellesiles, who perhaps has never read *Common Sense* (nor had any), of a willful intent to kill the Second Amendment. But all his distortion—prematurely but enthusiastically hailed by all the anti-gun media—cannot murder the Founding Fathers' wisdom in declaring that no law-abiding citizen be disarmed.

With Wayne LaPierre after Keynote address to the NRA in 2002.

When more astute historians began to really examine the Bellesiles book—which one early reviewer labeled as "the NRA's worst nightmare"—they discovered that the posturing professor had actually made up much of his so-called research. Just made it up out of the thin air of anti-gun bias. One of the most respected historians at Emory called the research "scholarly incompetence." To the university's credit, they asked Bellesiles to leave.

But that's the kind of thing those of us who think this part of our heritage should be preserved are up against. It is our duty to pass on to our children and grandchildren the wisdom of the Bill of Rights. That includes the Second Amendment as well as all the others.

If America is to remain the bright doorway of freedom for the world, we must be that shining portal for our children. That is our role and we are duty bound to serve its just cause. As another conservative Democrat once put it, "In the long history of the world, only a few generations have been granted the role of defending freedom in its hour of maximum danger. I do not shrink from this responsibility—I welcome it."

Those are the words of another NRA Life Member, President John F. Kennedy.

THE ENVIRONMENT, "PRISTINE," AND COMMON SENSE

14

I'm an environmentalist with a forty-year record to prove it. But just because I am an environmentalist doesn't mean I don't have common sense. When I came to Washington in the winter of my life, I discovered a species of environmentalist that is devoid of common sense. I call them the "extreme environmentalists."

As kind as I can say it, they are some of the most snobbish and sanctimonious people in a town filled with snobbish and sanctimonious people. Butter will not melt in their mouths. They are many and varied but the loudest—and the richest—include the Sierra Club and the League of Conservation Voters. I'm talking about their representatives inside the Beltway, not the rank-and-file members throughout this country. I could probably count on one hand those in Washington who are real outdoorsmen, the ones who would know the difference between a pine and a poplar, the ones who have, excuse me, ever "pee'd" in the woods. They are just more elite special interest groups, interested solely in winning elections and in raising money for carnivorous consultants to do the ultra-expensive work of shaping the image of some Playdough politician spouting their carefully crafted save-the-land, save this-or-that scripts.

President Clinton stated in his 1999 State of the Union address, "Our environment is the cleanest in twenty-five years." You tend to forget that pronouncement because the environmental elite, joined at the hip with the media, never gives you the good news about the environment. Believe it or not, in my native state of Georgia, the tenth-largest and third-fastest-growing state, even with all the industrial and residential development, the environment is in better shape than it was one hundred years ago by several measures. There are three million more acres of forest than a century ago. There are almost as many wetlands as in colonial days. If you don't want to take my word for it, read H. Harold Brown's myth-shattering book, *The Greening of Georgia*. The distinguished University of Georgia scholar maintains, "Georgia's air and water are cleaner today than they have been in fifty years." Should we continue to work to improve it? Of course.

In order to justify their existence, these Washington environmental groups regularly adopt some project they can manipulate into a highly visible, highly emotional fund-raising crusade, never mind if it's wildly impractical. Opposing the drilling for oil in a speck of the Arctic National Wildlife Refuge or ANWR is the latest of these and falls into the "lack of common sense" category.

Do the math. Follow the logic. We import 60 percent of America's energy from foreign sources that fix the price and do not have our country's best interests at heart. By 2010 this percentage will rise to 66. If we imported that much of the food we eat, people would be marching on Washington yelling that it is unacceptable because food is essential to our lives and to our national security. I don't believe they would accept some well-fed fool in Washington telling them to solve this problem by just not eating as much. Over the last two decades our economy has grown more than 125 percent, but our energy consumption has increased by only 30 percent. Nevertheless, the gap between supply and demand has grown.

The only way out of this dark valley is a broad-based energy policy that has a strong focus on conservation and efficiency. We should increase America's investment in domestic energy production. We need new technology that will produce clean coal energy.

With a quarter of the world's supply, we have been called the "Saudi Arabia of coal." Our supply is large enough to last more than 300 years. What we have to do is make its use cleaner, and that technology is rapidly reaching the point at which it can remove 90 percent of the harmful pollutants of sulfur dioxide, nitrogen oxide, and carbon dioxide. The word *nuclear* scares people who don't understand its great potential. We can have safe, efficient nuclear energy.

We need to get in touch with reality when it comes to resources found in the small part of northern Alaska known as ANWR. Debates rage over this barren stretch found, quite literally, at the end of the earth. According to the geologists, ANWR holds upwards of 16 billion barrels of oil. That's the equivalent of more than thirty years of imports of Saudi Arabian oil. It is the single best prospect for future domestic production. When people consider this proposition emotionally, in their mind's eye they see a wilderness turned into old Texas, with erector set dinosaurs nibbling away every square inch of land. Not so. With available new technology the entire footprint of oil drilling would be less than three square miles in total or about the size of Dulles Airport. Three square miles out of the entire ANWR area, which itself is about the size of South Carolina.

I have personally met with the native people who live in the area. They overwhelmingly support exploration. They believe the wildlife and environment they have depended on for tens of thousands of years can coexist with today's advanced technology.

ANWR is near the Prudhoe Bay oil field at the top of the Trans Alaska Pipeline. I've been there and seen it up close. For more than thirty years, that system has safely provided the U.S. with more than 20 percent of our domestically produced oil. None of the dire predictions about it has come true. From the $2.15 billion in federal royalties, the ANWR plan would also provide, in addition to oil, $2 billion directly to the states for land and water conservation.

But wait, the groups with the Sierra Club and the League of Conservation Voters leading the way, have made this the latest fund-raising crusade for their Charlie McCarthy candidates. It is their pet white mouse, one they have named "Pristine." They declare that pretty "Pristine" is about to be mutilated and must be saved from a cruel, ignorant, uncaring bunch of capitalist fat cats. But "Pristine," you see, is nothing but a fund-raising pet, pure and simple. And does "Pristine" bring in the money! The Sierra Club's donations went from $23.1 million to $67.1 million in a two-year period. Nine other organizations in the movement received total contributions of $330 million in 2001, up almost $100 million from the previous reporting period.

Like a pet mouse most people will never even see, "Pristine" is available mainly through snapshots and secondhand tales of her beauty and personality. If you wanted to take your family to see this pet, to see if it lived up to what you have heard, the cost to your family for the trip would be enormous. First, you'd have to drive or fly commercially to Fairbanks, Alaska. From there, you have to charter a small single engine plane to Arctic Village, a tiny Eskimo Community. That plane would be crowded for a family of four, but you're not even there yet. At Arctic Village, you'd have to charter still another "bush" plane to fly you over the Chandalar River Pass in the vast Brooks Range, an hour and a half flight, and often, planes can't get through because of heavy fog or blizzards.

"Pristine" is only viewable a few months out of the year and the weather often gets to 50 degrees below zero. Now, I'm no travel agent, but I believe the Grand Canyon, Yellowstone, Niagara Falls,

Cumberland Island, or countless other places would be more educational and certainly less expensive for a family vacation. But do you think these elitists even think about how few Americans might even want to make such a trip? Or could afford it? Of course they don't; they think everyone is on a liberal expense account like they are. How arrogant. "Pristine" is thousands of miles away at a place where hard-working families could never afford to visit. These all-knowing people always understand what's best for us; they always know what we should like, what we should drive, and even in this case, what we should think is pretty. Well, I'm sorry, I've seen "Pristine" up close. I think it's not that pretty. I believe the little mouse should be used in another way to help future generations.

What gives me the right to make these harsh analogies, you ask? Well, I thought you would never ask. My record gives me the right.

As I have noted in previous chapters, the way I think about things today can be traced back to how I was raised and where I was raised. Where I was raised has left me with a never-ending appreciation for the bounty of the land as well as its beauty.

In 1836, after General Winfield Scott had rounded up the Chattahooschee Indians to remove them to Indian Territory, the state of Georgia sent in surveyors to chart this new mountain area, to see exactly what they had acquired. Two of them, John Shaw and George Kellog, described one of the valleys in this way:

> Here is perhaps the most splendid mountain scenery upon the face of the globe—an amphitheater of probably 50 miles in circuit is formed by the Brasstown mountains and encircling a beautiful and fertile valley about four miles across interspersing with limpid streams and making upon the whole a picture unsurpassed and rarely if ever to be equaled for the wildness and grandeur of its scenery.

Before the two had written this in their "Cherokee Evaluations," and before the Trail of Tears was headed westward, my great-great-grandfather had come down out of the mountains of North Carolina and was waiting on the other side for the new territory to open up. As soon as it was legal, he crossed over the rugged terrain and moved his large family into the area. Our family has been there ever since. I was born and still live in that valley so beautifully described by Kellog and Shaw and have spent my life fishing its streams, walking its ridges, and climbing its summits. I've also spent considerable effort and political capital working to protect its environment.

Young Harris is at the base of Brasstown Bald Mountain, the highest peak in the state, and my mother hiked the rugged eight miles, some of it almost straight up, to the top more than a hundred times, once carrying my sister, then six months old, in her arms. I first climbed it when I was nine.

Two-thirds of the county I live in belongs to the federal government, the Tennessee Valley Authority, and the Chattahoochee National Forest. I'm glad. That's been great for preserving its natural beauty, and new wilderness areas have been added time and time again. But two-thirds is quite enough, thank you. Don't get me wrong, I believe in setting aside unusual, scenic geographic areas for those who come after us to enjoy. In 1961, when I was a newly elected state senator, the first bill I introduced was to set up a commission to study "the preservation of certain natural areas" in the state. About the same time, I took heavy criticism from my North Georgia neighbors because I opposed the extension of the Blue Ridge Parkway into the mountains. In 1970, I lobbied hard to make the Georgia Coastal Marshlands Protection Act a reality by encouraging legislators to support the measure and the governor to sign it. As lieutenant governor, I took heavy criticism from many of my mountain neighbors for trying to pass a similar Mountain Protection Act that I thought would have safeguarded the mountains from overdevelopment. The opposition was so fierce that the bill was defeated. As governor, one of my major initiatives harked back to my early idea of "protecting and setting aside certain natural areas" of the state. I called it Preservation 2000.

My goal, as it had been years before, was to acquire and protect 100,000 acres of national and environmentally sensitive land. Unaltered old growth forests and wetlands, including river bottoms, hard wood forests, bays, and other naturally occurring water features, were priority acquisitions under the program. By the end of my two terms, 105,602 acres at fifty-six locations were set aside at a cost of $122 million. Two of its most impressive areas are Tallulah Gorge, a spectacular chasm two miles long and a 1,000 feet deep, and Smithgall Woods, a spectacular 5,562 acres of lush mountain forests and trout streams.

My River Care 2000 initiative protects Georgia's 70,000 miles of streams and rivers. This ambitious program had three goals: assess important river and stream resources, identify effective management tools for river corridors, and acquire riverfront property for preservation. Almost $50 million went into this program.

In 1975, Governor Jimmy Carter established the Georgia Heritage Trust Act. My administration was able to increase Carter's original four sites of 27,000 acres dedicated to heritage preserves to 108 sites totaling more than 254,000 acres.

We strengthened the Costal Marshlands Act and the Shore Protection Act by substantially raising the level of protection for the coastal sand dunes, beach, sandbar, and shoals, which comprise the vital natural resources system known as the Sand Sharing System. The mighty Altamaha River, named as one of the last great places on Earth, benefited from our passage of the Protection of Tidewaters/Right of Passage Act and we cleared its banks of unsightly structures on its magnificent rush to the sea.

There were no certified landfill operators in Georgia when I became governor but when I left office there were 625, and more than 99.9 percent of the state's population was covered by a solid waste management plan. I created the Pollution Prevention Assistance Division, which offered technical assistance to businesses to reduce, reuse, and recycle materials and to lower demand for raw materials, water, and energy. I created a Solid Waste Trust Fund to fund the clean up of existing dumps, especially 300 significant tire dumps containing more than 5 million discarded tires. By the end of my administration, 4 million tires had been cleaned up, we had banned the dumping of tires, and a new EPD-approved recycling process was under way for 10.5 million scrap tires a year.

A particularly hard battle was passage of the Georgia Hazardous Site Response Act. We identified and inventoried 400 hazardous sites, and when we could identify the contaminators, we forced them to clean them up. We had to go toe to toe with many powerful business groups not only to pass the legislation but also to implement it. What made it so difficult was that many of these sites had been abandoned and the original violators were dead or long gone. Through fees, fines, and appropriations, a trust fund of more than $60 million was set up to help accomplish this.

Suffice it to say that on this subject, my credentials for more than four decades offer a pretty good public record. No brag, just fact. All along the way, I worked with some of the most dedicated men and women that can be found anywhere in the environmental movement, truly some of God's chosen few, working to protect and preserve this wondrous earth He gave us. We held fund-raisers—many of them—but I'll guarantee you this: none of the money ever went to candidates. It went to improve the environment. That's common sense.

THE ARTS, THE OPRY, AND A BABY'S BRAIN

15

Educational reform is getting a lot of attention these days. But rarely are the arts even mentioned as part of those efforts. The arts are too often considered a nice frill at the edge of the curriculum if you have extra time and resources, but the first thing you cut if you're going to get serious about education.

The arts are where I part company with many of my conservative friends. I believe the arts should be taught in school and there should be a division of government with a budget to promote them. Many conservatives do not favor a program like the National Endowment for the Arts. But the problem isn't with the concept of such a program, the problem is with the screwed up people who have tried to use the NEA to push their personal bad taste onto mainstream America.

For example, who was not repulsed and offended by the NEA-sponsored photograph of Robert Mapplethorpe with a bullwhip stuck up his rectum? It gives new meaning to "showing one's ass." Should taxpayer money be used to display that to a viewing public?

Of course not! And a better use for that bullwhip could have been found, like applying it to shoulders of the members who made that decision and some others just about as bad.

We tend to think of art as something done by a small group of talented people who have a special gift. But art is not just for artists. Art is for everyone. It is not a luxury, but a necessity that needs to be an integral part of our educational process. Art is essential to the preservation of the very fabric of our society. Biologically we are still cavemen. There is nothing of civilization contained in human genes. No language skills, no knowledge of history or literature, no understanding of the great truths of life, no comprehension of even who we are or how we got to be that way—none of this is contained in DNA. There is nothing automatic about the transfer of these things from one generation to the next. Yet that transfer must be made because the arts have rightly been called, "the signature of humankind."

Certainly, the arts, in their various forms, are a rich part of our identity. We are united as a people and a nation by the stories, myths, and beliefs we share. Those stories provide a common base of understanding and are told in this nation's artwork, music, drama, and literature.

We can also learn about other cultures by studying their artwork, music, dance, and literature. In fact, the arts help us to understand that truth is too big to be contained by any one culture, that there are underlying truths and principles that go beyond culture and tradition and unite humankind around the world and across the ages. We have to instill these critical concepts in our children who are growing up in a new global age. It is imperative they have a greater understanding and appreciation for cultural diversity.

But in addition to creating and nurturing our identity as a culture and giving us a framework for understanding other cultures, the arts also create and nurture our identity as individuals, enriching and bringing joy to our lives. We all say we want the next generation of children to understand their cultural heritage, to recognize and appreciate beauty, to have a healthy self-image, to be creative in their own expression, and to exercise higher-level critical thinking skills. Well, that's what art does. Art in the school curriculum will invest life with the meaning that makes the rest of learning and human endeavor worthwhile.

Participation in the arts strengthens children's academic skills because art is a problem-solving experience. You have to decide what results you want, then figure out how to put the parts together to create the overall effect you're after. Visual arts give children a hands-on feel for geometric shapes and spatial relationships. Auditory arts improve their listening skills and comprehension. Dramatic arts improve their communication skills. The College Entrance Examination Board has said that students who have participated in the arts at school score higher on the SAT. Researchers found in Georgia that middle and high school students with high levels of participation in the arts have lower dropout rates, score better on achievement tests, and are more likely to go to college.

Here's a fact most of us can appreciate: art is good for the economy and our wallets. One of my jobs as governor was to encourage new business facilities to locate in Georgia. CEOs of prospective companies unfailingly asked, "Is there a good museum, an orchestra, a ballet company, an arts festival?" That illusive "quality of life" factor has become vital to economic growth.

I like most kinds of music. Today, I favor bluegrass and classical. I've tried to listen to the catchy rhyme patterns of rap or hip-hop, but its vulgarity, violence, and evil intent cut too deeply into my sensitivity for any real appreciation. In fact, this powerful tool of expression disturbs me greatly because I believe, as someone has said, songwriters influence what society thinks more than politicians. Today, that may not be good coming from either direction.

My first introduction to music and its hypnotic affect came from a Silvertone radio my mother bought from Sears & Roebuck. It sat on a table in our living room and from that magic box with four knobs and a greenish dial came many wondrous sounds but none that touched me more deeply nor endured so long as the ones I got by turning the dial to 650 on Saturday nights.

WSM Radio was a 50,000-watt clear-channel station and was one of the few stations one could get in the mountains at night. I remember pouring water on the ground wire to make the music come in clearer, and other times just sitting there with the ground wire in my hands. It was worth it because this was where I could hear the Grand Ole Opry, which began in 1925 and today is the longest continuous radio program in history.

Country music once was a large part of my existence, and I used to spend a lot of time in Music City USA, Nashville, Tennessee. I am a fan of the old country music when it was, as songwriter legend Harlan Howard described it, "three cords and the truth." Today's new acts don't do much for me. There are some exceptions, like Vince Gill, Alan Jackson, and Patty Lovelace. Vince's "When I Call Your Name" is a classic and I want his "Go Rest High on That Mountain" played at my funeral. You can't get much bigger than Alan Jackson in height, talent, or acclaim. He's a giant who can catch the feeling of Middle America better than the best pollster and a hundred focus groups. Witness his song "The Little Man" and his thoughts on September 11, 2001, "Where Were You When the World Stopped Turning."

Many of the artists and songwriters were and are among my most cherished friends. Hall of Famer Bill Anderson of Georgia has been a close friend for forty years. Ronnie Milsap was my bright student at Young Harris College. Jan Howard campaigned for me as far back as 1966. George Jones, the greatest country singer of them all, made the best television spot I've ever had when I ran for governor in 1990. Known at one time in his long career as "No Show" Jones for missing concert dates, he ended this spot with "And this is one election I'm going to show up for."

There are so many, many others I claim as friends. Among them are the late Waylon Jennings and his wonderful wife, Jessi Coulter,

With George Jones, the greatest country music singer of them all.

Charley Pride, Dickie Lee, Brenda Lee, Jean Sheperd, and Randy Travis. No one was happier to see the recognition that Dr. Ralph Stanley received with *Brother Where Art Thou* than I. There also was the late Johnny Russell, and many others too numerous to mention who own a corner of my heart. And there is the genius producer and songwriter, Jack Clement, who spent more nights with me at the Governor's Mansion than anyone outside my immediate family.

I must mention the late Tammy Wynette. I first met Tammy in 1966 when she came to Blairsville, Georgia, to do a show for my congressional campaign. Bill Anderson and I had toured ten cities the Saturday before. He and his band would play and sing and I'd speak and we'd move on. We had missed Blairsville and they wanted some Grand Ole Opry music themselves; after all, they were my neighbors. Bill couldn't come but he called and said he had a really good "girl singer" that would come. "No one has ever heard of her, but she's got a set of lungs. They'll like her. Her name is Tammy Wynette."

She was even better than Bill had promised. I paid her with a $150 check and I could tell she examined it carefully. It was made on the Bank of Hiawassee, so when she made her way through Hiawassee, a few miles away, she stopped and went in to the bank. She walked up to a teller and said, "I've got this check on this local politician; I'd like to cash it while I'm in town. I hope it's good." The teller counted out $150 in cash and introduced herself, "I'm Shirley Miller, and he's my husband." Two weeks later, a record called *Apartment Number 9* began to climb the charts. The artist was that unknown Tammy Wynette, and she was on her way.

We saw each other often over the years as she became a huge star and I slowly climbed the political ladder and we would laugh about that day. When I ran for governor in 1990, one of the top events of my campaign in South Georgia was Tammy Wynette and Randy Travis. I didn't speak. I just stood on the stage with a silly grin on my face as she held my hand and sang "Stand By Your Man."

Another great friend who has passed on was Mae Boren Axton, who wrote "Heartbreak Hotel" for Elvis. She was Hoyt Axton's mother and the aunt of former U.S. Senator David Boren.

I especially love and admire songwriters and their ability to create a mood, to make you happy or sad, to cause you to think, to tell you a three-minute story that is as lasting as what Hemingway took 300 pages to do is one of the greatest talents anyone could have. I even wrote a book back in the 1980s titled *They Heard*

Georgia Singing. I told the stories of hundreds of musical greats from my state—Ray Charles, Otis Redding, Lena Horne, Alan Jackson, Travis Tritt, Jessye Norman, Little Richard, to name a few.

Here's how the thought of integrating music into the learning process of children came about. In the nearly fifty years Shirley and I have been married, we have been blessed with the opportunity to watch, up close, three generations of little ones—our own two children, four grandchildren, and four great-grandchildren. I have always been amazed how quick and agile their minds are during this early period of their lives—more than at any other time. They absorbed liked little sponges everything they saw and heard—including some things you might not want them to absorb. It fascinated me, so I read everything I could find on the subject. It inspired me to create Georgia's statewide pre-kindergarten program for four-year-olds.

I was especially spellbound a few years ago by a special edition of *Newsweek* that revealed intriguing details and theories on how a baby's brain develops. I found like-minded interests as I served at chairman of the Education Commission of the States. So we held a national conference in Georgia on brain development and how tiny children learn. During this process, I began to learn more and more about the role music can play in learning.

We all accept the value of music as a tool for managing mind, body, and mood. Music can help us relax, or it can help to stimulate and invigorate us. It can create a romantic mood, a melancholy mood, or lift our spirits when we're dragging. It can even put us into the proper frame of mind to concentrate and focus our minds, so that we can learn more readily and achieve at higher levels.

The next obvious question is whether the positive impact of music on learning extends down into the earliest years or even months when the brain is first developing. We have always tended to measure the development of our babies based on their eyes, watching for their eyes to come into better focus and for hand-eye coordination to evolve. But the ear is actually the first sensory organ to develop. Unborn babies begin to hear just sixteen weeks into pregnancy. And hearing is pretty much the unborn baby's only stimulation from the outside world as its brain begins to develop.

Research suggests that sounds have a direct connection to brain development. The first sound unborn babies hear is their mother's heartbeat and the corresponding rhythmic whoosh of blood in the placenta. And throughout life we tend to enjoy music most when its rhythms move at the same tempo as our heartbeat. By the time a baby is born, its hearing is so sophisticated it can differentiate between a recording of its mother's prenatal womb sounds and the sounds of another baby's mother. Newborns also recognize the emotional content in the recording of their mother's womb sounds and respond with movements and changes in their own heart rate.

We also know that a baby's brain continues to form after birth, not just growing bigger as toes and fingers do, but developing more and more microscopic connections that will be responsible for learning and remembering throughout life. At birth, a baby has 100 billion or more neurons forming more than 50 trillion connections, or synapses. But during the first several months of life, that number increases twenty times to more than 1,000 trillion. And it is these mental maps—these patterns and connections that are made and reinforced in the brain during the early months and years of life—that form the basis of our intelligence.

Research shows that reading and talking with an infant, especially having that infant listen to soothing music, helps those trillions of brain connections to develop, especially the ones related to math. You see, what underlies our spatial reasoning skills is our ability to detect and predict patterns. And that is what musical melodies and harmonies are—sequences of sound patterns that strengthen the brain's ability to process information and identify patterns.

As early as four months old, babies will react to changes in melodies. As young as six months old, they can detect notes that are out of tune, and some can sing back to you a pitch that you've sung to them. This is not theory; it is fact.

The brain has two lobes, or hemispheres. The left hemisphere controls analytical, logical, and language skills. The right hemisphere controls visual skills, direct perception, and creativity. People are sometimes called right- or left-brain thinkers depending on whether they tend to think intuitively or logically. Music, however, engages both hemispheres. Its creativity and ability to evoke emotions engages the right hemisphere. But the mechanics of deciphering melody, rhythm, and pitch intervals belong to the left. It's reasonable to conclude from research that people who receive musical exposure and training early in life when their brain circuits are still developing have a larger "corpus callosum," the bundle of nerves connecting the logic of the left hemisphere with the creativity and insight of the right.

Because I had come to believe in the importance of music's relation to learning, I developed the idea of somehow exposing Georgia's babies to more music. I'd had it in the back of my mind for about a year, but I couldn't figure out how to do it.

The idea began to come clear when I was at the hospital the day my granddaughter took our second great-grandchild home. She was given this big bag of samples—diapers, wipes, baby formula, baby food. A new thought flashed in my head: the state of Georgia could put a CD or a tape in here with a little information for parents about how they could begin to build the power of their baby's brain through music. It would be an easy thing they could do to help their little ones develop. When, as governor, I proposed this, the national and international attention it attracted amazed me.

Most of it was positive, but some objected to using tax dollars. As I thought about it, I could see their point. Fortunately, at the same time, I was hearing from some large and well-known recording companies interested in helping. The first was Sony Music Entertainment, whose manufacturing plant in Carrollton, Georgia, was the largest in the world. It was a natural move to involve them.

The next consideration was choosing the music. I know what I like to listen to. But I was unsure of my ability to choose the proper music for babies. Then Michael Maguire, Tony Award-winning tenor who sings both on Broadway and in opera, came to perform at a cultural event at the Governor's Mansion. He had read about my idea and was enthusiastic, because he is exposing his own two small children to music. So he and Joe Laskey of Sony helped me put the musical selections together. It includes eleven selections from Beethoven, Mozart, Handel, Bach, Schubert, and Antonio Vivaldi, who wrote much of his music for young girls in an Italian orphanage. Two selections that I insisted on including were "Jesu, Joy of Man's Desiring" from Bach's Cantata No. 147 and Beethoven's "Für Elise."

Now, the parents of every baby born in a Georgia hospital take home either a cassette tape or a CD titled "Build Your Baby's Brain through the Power of Music." This is the message I sent to the parents on the cover of the CD or tape:

> It really works! Einstein knew it. So did Galileo. They knew that there was a direct relationship between music and math. What many studies have shown since is that the connection begins in infancy and can be increased by a baby hearing soothing music on a regular basis.
>
> A six-month-old infant can tell whether music is harmonious or not. Microscopic connections in the brain responsible for learning and remembering are enhanced through listening.
>
> That, my dear parent, is why Sony Music and I wanted you to have this recording. Play it often. I hope both you and your baby enjoy it—and that your little one will get off to a smart start.

"GIVE TO BIGOTRY NO SANCTION"

16

Civil rights have been the great issue of my time and I cannot help thinking I've lived long enough to watch history come full circle. When I was a young state senator arguing that race should not matter, I was considered a liberal. Now, forty years later, when I am an old U.S. senator and argue that race should not matter, I'm considered a conservative.

But my concern with race and the way it permeates so many aspects of life in America began even before I began to weigh its political consequences.

In 1948 I was a junior in high school. I was selected by my class-mates to make one of six speeches on George Washington's birthday. One winner would be chosen from this annual chapel exercise that was mandatory for all students. At that time, still more interested in baseball than public speaking or even girls, I was lured into this knee-knocking experience by my English teacher, Miss Edna Herren, for whom I would have gladly jumped off a cliff had she suggested it.

I sweated bullets as I practiced and practiced. I had chosen as my topic the unlikely subject of civil rights. There had been a lot of talk at our home around the radio and kitchen table since Harry Truman first advocated his far-reaching program that included abolition of segregation in the armed forces, a Fair Employment Practices Commission, abolition of the poll tax, making lynching a federal crime, and outlawing discrimination in interstate travel. My family was for it.

I'll never forget my opening line, "Civil rights—perhaps no phrase in recent times has been so much used and so little understood." For the next seven minutes, I laid out my case for the judges, a local legislator and two businessmen. My eloquence and the touchy subject failed to move them in my direction . . . or Truman's. Someone else got the prize.

That speech on George Washington's birthday was just words. I was a white boy in a predominantly white county. I knew just a handful of people whose skin was a different color. Four years later, I begin to experience what it was like to live and work with people whose backgrounds were different from mine. In August 1953, Platoon 311 at the Marine Recruit Depot at Parris Island, South Carolina, was our own little melting pot housed in one crowded Quonset hut, all types, all classes and races. It did not take us long to understand that we would sink or swim together. At that time not a one of us had heard of Martin Luther King Jr., but we would come to understand what he articulated later. "We must live together as brothers or perish together as fools."

We lived together as brothers and bonded so tightly that the brotherhood still exists today with all Marines whether they were in that Quonset hut or not.

So, by my first year in the state senate in 1961, I had a different perspective than I would have had I not been a Marine. The annual session opened in chaos. Federal Judge William Bootle had issued a decision, breaking down the racial barriers at the University of Georgia. His order admitted two African-Americans, Hamilton

Holmes and Charleyne Hunter. Georgia Governor Ernest Vandiver had been elected in 1958 after promising there would be no integration of the University. "No not one," he would say to thunderous applause. Those three words would haunt him. On the evening before the first day of the session, I told a reporter from the *Atlanta Journal*, "Integration is not the worst that can happen. Locking the doors of the University is the worst thing."

At first only a handful of legislators felt that way and numerous bills were introduced to maintain segregation. The first one in the Senate was a bill from the governor that would allow Georgia students to forego school if African-Americans were enrolled. Only four of the fifty-four senators spoke against it. I was one. When they tried to pass it with a voice vote instead of a show of hands, I objected and asked to be recorded as voting "no."

As the days went by, Governor Vandiver began to change his mind. He was hearing from, among others, Robert Woodruff, the legendary head of Coca-Cola, and Griffin Bell, the respected attorney who was close to Vandiver and would later be named a federal judge by President John Kennedy and attorney general by Jimmy Carter. Finally, the governor went before a joint session of the Legislature and asked us to keep the university open. At that time, it was an extremely brave thing for him to do and I've always admired him for it. Unlike Alabama and Arkansas, Georgia integrated its schools peacefully. Carl Sanders, who served in the Senate at that time, was elected governor two years later in a race against former governor and arch-segregationist Marvin Griffin. I strongly supported Sanders and later served in that progressive administration.

So Miller was a courageous racial moderate at a time in the South when they were scarce, right? Wrong! If only that were the whole story. If only I could have continued on that road I began as a teenager. Regrettably, my spine turned to jelly. Like one of the rats that followed the Pied Piper into the river to die, I followed the Pied

Piper into the quicksand of political expediency. I will regret my words for the rest of my life.

In 1964, I ran for Congress against the incumbent Phil Landrum in a campaign that I thought would be a battle over federal aid to education. Landrum was against it. I was for it. But it was not to be that simple. In politics, few things are. In the middle of the campaign, President Johnson named Landrum House leader to author his War on Poverty Act. There was plenty of poverty in our mountain district. Johnson even came into the heart of the district and endorsed Landrum. The *Atlanta Constitution* ran a cartoon of Landrum on Johnson's shoulder, and in the background, obviously run over by them, was a crew-cut wannabe on the ground holding a sign saying "Something New." That was me.

But that's not the point of this story. The point is that it was 1964 and the Civil Rights Bill was an issue with especially strong opposition in the South. Almost automatically, all those running said they were against it. Including me. I even proclaimed that there should be an "investigation of Communist infiltration in the civil rights movement." What an idiot!

Only one Georgia congressman had the guts to support the bill. That was Charles Weltner of Atlanta, who later became a great Georgia Supreme Court chief justice. He had the integrity I sadly lacked. My words and actions have tormented me ever since.

To make it even worse, after President Johnson came with his juggernaut, I responded, "Johnson is a Southerner who has sold his birthright for a mess of dark porridge." The minute it was out of my mouth I regretted it, and I've regretted this whole sordid episode ever since. It has been a source of shame I have never been able to escape. I only hope that the totality of my forty-year record since then is proof that they were the words of someone who at that time was a political weakling, but not a racist.

After that, I worked for three consecutive governors, Carl Sanders, Lester Maddox, and Jimmy Carter, all very different. I had served in the state senate with Sanders and Carter but had never

Twenty-five years ago in the Georgia Senate with Julian Bond, now NAACP president.

met nor voted for Maddox until he called me into his office one day from where I had been working as assistant commissioner in the Department of Corrections. He asked me to be his executive secretary during the forty-day legislative session.

The forty days turned into two years. He didn't say anything about me going back to corrections, and I didn't either. It turned out to be a good experience. Even though Maddox had been elected as a segregationist, for the first time the state patrol was integrated, as were the county welfare offices throughout the state. The first African-American was appointed to a major state board. Julian Bond recalls that when he was a state senator, he asked Maddox to put African-Americans on local draft boards and "Just like that, he did it. He didn't have to study it or anything."

Later, I was a leader in making Martin Luther King Jr.'s birthday a holiday in Georgia. I appointed the first African-American female to the State Supreme Court, and, at the time, the only African-American as attorney general in the nation, and another as commissioner of labor. In fact, I appointed more African-Americans to the state judiciary and constitutional offices than all the previous governors of Georgia combined. I also tried in 1993, long before the NAACP boycotts were threatened, to change the Georgia flag with its confederate "St. Andrews" cross. I'm proud—and humbled—that in all eight of my statewide races, civil rights leaders such as John Lewis, Julian Bond, Maynard Jackson, David Scott, Hank Aaron, M. L. ("Daddy") King Sr., Shirley Franklin, and Andrew Young all stood with me.

Over and over, I've said and truly believe that the Civil Rights Act was the most important legislation in my lifetime. It has changed my state and this nation in so many positive ways. I will go to my grave regretting my position on it in 1964 and my terrible words in a fit of frustration and anger. Tattooed on my brain forever are those lines from *The Rubaiyat* of Omar Khayyam, "The moving finger writes and having writ, moves on. And all man's piety, tears, and wit cannot erase a single line." How very true. Nothing I have done or can do will ever "erase" what I did. But what that brief moment of weakness forty years ago did was to cause me to study, observe, and give a lot of thought to the issue of intolerance in this country.

After World War II, Winston Churchill remarked in a speech, "How much we have done. How much we still have to do." So it is with unity and community in America. Gone are the days when African-Americans in my state of Georgia were denied access to lunch counters. Gone are the days when Japanese Americans were herded into camps because we were at war with Japan. But how much we still have to do.

In Washington and back in the red clay hills of Georgia, all of us continue to struggle with that simple question Rodney King asked a decade ago: "Can we all get along?" That incident, and what followed, posed a daunting challenge. That shocking videotape raised the question of whether those four policemen were able to see beyond the color of Rodney King's skin. Later, we wondered whether it was the color of their skin that took precedence in the mind of that jury when it failed to convict those officers of excessive force.

But then, in the violence that followed, we saw the same thing in the other direction. People were attacked and injured simply because they were white. Some of those protestors, like the policemen, like that jury, did not look beyond the color of skin. When that happens, we deny the other person's humanity. We deny the fact that there is a fellow human being underneath that skin.

The aim of the great struggle in the 1960s was to achieve civil rights. That was the right place to begin. And we must continue to guard against those injustices. But on the opposite side of the same coin are economic rights. That is really our challenge today.

For example, as a result of the civil rights movement, African-Americans can now sit wherever they want on the bus, but almost four out of ten of their children are born in poverty. As a result of the civil rights movement, African-Americans can now use whatever drinking fountain or restroom is most convenient, but their rates of unemployment are double that of whites. As a result of the civil rights movement, African-Americans can now eat at the restaurant of their choice, but their infants die at a rate twice that of whites.

You see, America has not yet addressed the economic side of the coin.

I grew up poor but I grew up with hope. I grew up with my single parent drilling into me that if I worked hard and played by the rules I could get somewhere, I could become somebody. "Being somebody" was important in that home I grew up in. One of my earliest memories was my mother telling me the story of "The Little Engine that Could."

But today, many Americans have no hope. They have no hope of escaping poverty, no hope of taking control of their own destiny, no hope of becoming somebody.

The social programs created in the 1960s were designed to compensate the victims of poverty rather than solve the problems that cause it. They gave poor people just enough in the way of Medicaid, welfare, food stamps, and housing subsidies to keep and sustain them in their poverty instead of giving them the skills and opportunities they needed to break out of their poverty.

The world has undergone tremendous change since the 1960s. The industrial age, on which those old social programs were modeled, has given way to a new era of microelectronics, satellites, and fiber-optic cables—a world of modern technology. Today the critical infrastructure required to generate economic growth is intellectual. We have a more educated, more highly skilled workforce. We must change from spending money to sustain people in their poverty to investing that money in training, educating, and providing them with economic opportunity.

That must be part of any additional welfare reform. I introduced a bill in the U.S. Senate to create a commission to work on new ways to eliminate "persistent poverty" in the old "Black Belt" of the Southeast. About 7.5 million people live in this region composed of 242 counties in seven states. One of every four residents is under eighteen. The region comprises predominantly white residents, but the percentage of African-Americans is three times the percentage of those living throughout the United States. Along with its high poverty rate, the region has a disproportionate share of social ills in education, birth rates, disease, housing, and unemployment. Its economy lacks an able workforce and the tools with which to build wealth.

Theodore Roosevelt once said that "this country will not be a good place for any of us to live in unless we make it a good place for all of us to live in." Today, half of those who enter the workforce are African-American, Asian, Hispanic, or of Middle Eastern descent.

What all of us have got to realize pretty quickly is that we are all Americans. The greater the social and economic equity among us, the less likely we are to face escalating problems of race.

Each generation must adapt to the needs of our changing racial mix. There was a time, for example, when affirmative action could easily be justified. All at once, we were taking a large group of people and, in effect, saying, you now have an opportunity to participate in our national marathon. Come on up to the starting line and join in with these white folks who have been preparing for years for this big race. Never mind that your legs have become cramped from those shackles you've been wearing for years. Just go to it; you can now enter that marathon just like everybody else.

But, you see, because of their past circumstances, in all fairness, they needed a little head start. They needed some time to get in shape just like all the other runners. The only fair and right thing to do was to give them some time to achieve better condition. Now, forty years and two generations have come and gone. For four decades affirmative action has had a laudable purpose and it provided time to prepare. But the time has come to modify it. Income level should now be the criteria for affirmative action, not the color of one's skin.

I hope that I can look back and say that I had some impact on economic and racial equality. I am proud that two of the people who made the most lasting impact on equality were fellow Georgians who have inspired me along with the world. Jackie Robinson's courageous integration of baseball in 1947 not only foreshadowed the civil rights movement, it paved the way. It laid the foundation on which the movement led by Dr. Martin Luther King Jr. was built.

Jackie was born in Grady County, near Cairo. I have visited his old homestead. Today only some of the foundation and a chimney remain. Shortly before his death in 1972, Jackie wrote, "A life is not important except in the impact it has on other lives." Today, we can only begin to guess the vastness of his impact on the millions of white Americans who had their horizons widened and the millions of African-Americans who had their opportunities expanded because of his life.

Armed with athletic skills and personal determination, Jackie Robinson pressed ahead in the face of bigotry, hatred, and loneliness. From the baseball diamond, he engaged a whole generation of Americans in a conversation on the nature of equal rights.

I mentioned this in another chapter but it is worth repeating. Two centuries ago, Moses Sesixas, Warden of the Hebrew Congregation of Newport, Rhode Island, wrote to the president of this new nation of his delight at the birth of "a government that gives to bigotry no sanction, to persecution no assistance, but generously affords to all, liberty of conscience." On the wall of my Senate office in the Dirksen Building, there is a copy of the historic letter that George Washington wrote back, affirming that the government of the United States would "give to bigotry no sanction, to persecution no assistance."

Can't we all try to live our lives by what we know deep in our hearts: that all men—and women—are created equal? All of us. We eat; we sleep. We have strengths and weaknesses; we have dreams and anxieties. A tear knows no race, no religion, no color. We all cry in the same language.

But freedom from prejudice and discrimination means more than tolerance, more than overlooking our differences. Instead, it celebrates our differences. Our diversity must become our greatest strength. Or our prejudices will become our crippling weakness.

Many years ago, the Rabbis were asked why was it that in the beginning God created just one man, Adam, and just one woman, Eve. Surely God could have created multitudes. The Rabbis said that only one man and one woman were created to help us all remember that we all come from the same mother and father. No one should ever say, "I'm better that you," and no one should ever feel, "I'm less than you."

Dr. Martin Luther King Jr. wrote to us from his jail cell in Birmingham: "We must come to see that human progress never rolls in on wheels of inevitability. It comes through the tireless efforts and persistent work of people willing to be coworkers with God . . . . Now is the time to make real the promise of democracy . . . . Now is the time to lift our national policy from the quicksand of racial injuries to the solid rock of human dignity."

Now is the time. Now is always the time.

"To Secure These Rights"

17

If government can't keep its citizens safe, it fails. It fails at its first basic purpose and anything else it accomplishes pales in comparison. That is what homeland security is about. It is why I fought to create a large, flexible separate department as President Bush recommended, and dismayed many of my Democratic brethren who failed to see the dangers of delay caused by partisan carping.

We have only to refer back to the Declaration of Independence to understand that the security of this country was top of mind with its framers. Most everyone is familiar with these words of our most memorable document: "We hold these truths to be self-evident: that all men are created equal, that they are endowed by their Creator with certain unalienable rights, that among them are life, liberty and the pursuit of happiness."

We all know those words. But do you know what the next sentence is? "That to secure these rights, governments are instituted among men, deriving their just powers from the consent of the governed." That is the reason we have government—"to secure," that is, to keep safe our rights.

On the morning of September 11, 2001, nineteen men armed with box cutters, the skill to pilot a jet airliner, and a fanatical zeal changed forever the meaning of keeping our citizens safe. In two hours, thousands of Americans were killed on our own soil and before our very eyes as we watched in horror.

One of the scariest things about today's terrorists is the difficulty in predicting how they will strike next. That frightening unknown is one of their greatest strengths. Seldom do they use the same mode of operation or the same weapons, although a variety of bombs have been used 87 percent of the time in almost 800 attacks against U.S. interests.

Recent intelligence warns us we now have to be aware that enemies are willing and may be able to use chemical weapons. We know that Saddam Hussein used the nerve gas sarin and mustard gas in more than 400 attacks over Kurdish towns in the late 1980s. Terrorists in 1995 released sarin in a Tokyo subway killing several and injuring more than 5,000.

As horrible as it is to contemplate, we must be prepared for the use of biological weapons like smallpox, anthrax, or ricin. The Russians had stocks of smallpox virus and we don't know where all of it is. We can't even be sure of random villains in our own country. The anthrax someone mailed to U.S. senators was so highly refined, odds are it was prepared in a U.S. government lab. So called "dirty bombs," made with radioactive materials obtained through underground contacts, can be transported in something as small as a suitcase.

So as horrible as 9/11 was, the potential for even worse attacks is real. The thought that it could happen on any day at anytime will hover over us for years. So in addition to deciding how America will cope with these attacks systematically, we must be able to cope psychologically. That said, an even greater fear for me is that we will become so immersed in partisan sniping we won't prepare adequately on either front and will appear divided and weak to our enemies. Seeking political advantage on this issue is like sending engraved invitations to our enemies to attack.

I'm sorry to say that several of the current Democratic presidential candidates have, in my opinion, crossed that line and I am alarmed that their heated campaign rhetoric is doing this country great harm in a time of peril. We need to be more united on this issue, not further divided.

Intelligence has been called "the long pole" in the tent of the campaign against terrorism. And we have seen how important it is to get it accurate. Our intelligence capabilities must be strengthened significantly. Someone dropped the ball by not warning that the hunt for the weapons of mass destruction could be a long and drawn-out process. The new kind of threats from terrorists and rogue nations make accurate intelligence even more important than in conventional warfare. I have great confidence in the Bush national security team and feel sure that they will use both the carrot and the stick to bring this about.

We also have to significantly increase the level of our resources. Presently, the emergency responders on state and local levels do not have the training, the equipment or the personnel to deal with a major attack if one were to take place. We have to forget the zealous guarding of little individual intelligence kingdoms and overhaul our systems to improve sharing of information. The overhaul should extend from all the different federal agencies down to the state and local levels. It's appalling how little information is shared among various agencies. That includes even sheriff's offices not sharing with other sheriff's offices or local police chiefs. Sometimes they stubbornly refuse to share; but more often they can't share because the radio frequencies and equipment aren't compatible. Presently, they have to go through a third party like a radio operator. Unfortunately, this cannot be corrected quickly and it will be very expensive.

One of the most daunting challenges is how to secure our 361 seaports where each year six million inbound containers arrive. In fact, 95 percent of all commerce coming into this country arrives through the seaport system. Containers are quickly unloaded and just as quickly dispersed around the country. They were not inspected before they left the foreign port, and only 2 percent are inspected when they arrive here. It is a disaster waiting to happen.

With mounting awareness of this potential peril, we passed the Maritime Transportation Act in November 2002. It laid out certain mandates such as requiring all ships coming in to U.S. ports to have long-range identification tracking systems and the electronic filing of cargo information. It also gives each port flexibility to craft a security plan that addresses the individual port. The Coast Guard has estimated it will take over $1 billion a year just to meet the baseline mandates.

Nevertheless, we don't have much choice, so how do we meet this huge new expense? For one thing, it may be necessary to implement a user fee on cargo shippers similar to the one on airline passengers in order to pay for the expansion of inspections. Forgetting for a moment the threats to human life, just consider the disruption to business that would be caused by a terrorist act at one or more of our ports. In 2002 when labor strikes shut down twenty-nine ports on the West Coast for ten days, it cost the U.S. economy millions of dollars a day. A major point of their disagreement was that the new electronic cargo tracking technology is expected to make some water front jobs obsolete, and the union wanted jurisdiction on new jobs.

While we are tightening security, we need to face the reality of dealing with the more than ten million illegal aliens in our country. Each year, 400,000 are entering our country. This is a huge and dangerous problem and no one in a position to do anything about it wants to do anything about it. Not the executive branch, not the legislative branch, not diplomats, not business, not labor, not educators, not farmers, not religious leaders, and especially not Democratic and Republican lawmakers. It is a bipartisan dereliction of duty. No one wants to do anything because no one wants to lose a few votes. It has become a high stakes contest between the leaders of both parties to see which one can pander the most. They should muster up the will to send illegal aliens back to where they came from. Instead both parties stumble all over themselves rushing to grant amnesty.

Our borders are so open to the illegal immigrants that their enablers in the United States had the unmitigated gall to demand the installation of water fountains along the way so the illegals won't get thirsty. Of course, like a fawning concierge, INS responded. Not only do they have water to drink but also what are called "rescue beacons" so that if these illegals need help they can just press a button to summon it.

The Canadian border is four thousand miles long and the Mexican border two thousand miles. We have about one border patrolman to about every ten miles. What kind of security is that? In one area alone, the St. Regis Mohawk Reservation in Upstate New York, some 4,000 illegal aliens cross the St. Lawrence River each year and are smuggled into New York City. We should send National Guardsmen to stop this illegal traffic on our borders. We send them to faraway places like Kosovo and Afghanistan to make these countries safer. What about us?

Legal immigration? Certainly. It's what helped make this country great. There are immigrants waiting in line to come into this country and they are obeying the law. Give them the chance to become American citizens, instead of the illegals who have made a mockery of the American Dream.

Illegal aliens cause monumental problems within our framework of social services. We are spending millions on their healthcare, schooling, criminal incarceration, and other entitlements that could be used to improve the life of American citizens. False IDs are easy to get and in most of our large cities, the local police are forbidden to ask them about their immigration status. It is illegal according to many local ordinances and even a special order (#40) from the INS. This has been the case in Los Angeles since 1979, and two months after 9/11, New York Republican mayor Michael Bloomberg put out this lunatic statement: "People who are undocumented do not have to worry about city government going to the federal government." Of course, he was only continuing what former Democratic mayor Ed Koch had put in place years before.

Unbelievable! We should be doing just the opposite. Anyone here illegally should be put in jail, his or her property forfeited, and immediately deported. An existing federal law calls for heavy fines for employers who knowingly hire illegal, but it is ignored. It should be strictly enforced. In fact, the federal government should require all employers to verify U.S. citizenship or lawful presence for each job application by a telephone or central database maintained by U.S. government.

Although the overwhelming number of illegal aliens are not criminals and have absolutely no connection to terrorists at all, the few that do are some really bad actors. Don't forget three of the September 11 hijackers were here illegally as were those who made the first attack on the World Trade Center. Lee Malvo, the young Washington, D.C. sniper is not only an illegal alien but one of many that had been in federal custody and released. Just like Maximilians Esparza from El Salvador, who had been arrested in both California and Oregon and stopped twice and released by the U.S. Border Patrol. He had raped two nuns and strangled one of them with her rosary beads. The list of examples is endless. Someday our grand-children are going to reap the results of this madness and wonder what in the world this nation and its leaders were thinking.

The list of what INS does not know is longer than the list of what INS does know. For example, it cannot tell you where the million "students" given a visa to attend college are actually enrolled in college or even where they are. Neither do they know how many criminal aliens are in jail or prison nationwide. They are supposed to be immediately deported after being released but they aren't. Think what it is costing our financially hard-strapped states to keep them in custody. It is hundreds of millions of dollars which they cannot afford. And when it comes to the cost of illegal immigration, we can't even take into account the displacement of American workers from their jobs.

This is not to say all our problems are caused by illegal aliens, or that all our terror comes from terrorists. The fear of crime was one of America's biggest worries before we were even aware of terrorism. Innocent people have been sitting behind burglar bars, virtual prisoners in their own homes. They are afraid of the criminals who ought to be behind real prison bars. They turn on the TV or read the paper and know that on any given day they could be hurt or killed or have treasured possessions stolen or damaged. They are afraid of child molesters, afraid some stranger will sell their children drugs, and afraid of becoming victims in a system that seems to focus more on the rights of criminals than on them.

How times have changed. In Young Harris you didn't even lock your doors at night; you didn't lock your car if you were lucky enough to have one. It was safe for children to walk to school, and it was safe for teachers to teach in school. Neighbors knew neighbors. That's the world I grew up in, and for most adults my age, that's the world they remember as well.

But, in recent years, violent thugs have affected the lives of all of us. We are all touched by the violence, even if we are not the actual victims. It is that uneasiness the late-night store clerk feels. It is the anxiety the secretary feels when she walks alone to the parking garage. It is the fear that shoots through the mom as she momentarily loses eye contact with her child in a busy mall, or that nervousness we've all shared when unknown footsteps walk behind us at night.

Ranking right along with fear is frustration. Good, decent, law-abiding citizens are frustrated by a criminal justice system they believe doesn't work, a system where a twenty-year sentence really means just a bunch of words on a piece of paper. Where criminals escape with plea bargains and serve no time. Where a system is more adept at letting criminals out than keeping criminals locked away. Our citizens simply don't feel justice is being served. I have the same frustration.

I am frequently asked two questions: Why don't violent criminals get tougher sentences? Most importantly, why don't violent criminals have to serve the time the judge gives them? Those questions deserve answers.

Law enforcement takes our officers into difficulties and dangers far exceeding any other era in our country. Terrorists, drug-related crimes, and an acceleration of just plain rage and meanness are imprinted on our daily thoughts. Officers face horrors in the line of duty that would make the rest of us cringe and turn away. Someone once said that the difference between a hero and a coward is one step sideways. No one understands that better than law enforcement officers who meet danger head-on, with no sidestepping. Their dedication to duty and their heroism deserves more than a judicial system that is more preoccupied with the rights of criminals than the rights of the victims or those who protect us.

Our judicial system was created to deal with those who break society's laws. Many of those who have been the targets of crime feel they have been victimized twice—first by the criminal and then by the judicial system.

As governor and now as senator, I have worked to bring the rights and needs of crime victims back into better balance. Today in Georgia, the victim's family in a capital felony case can appear before the court at the sentencing stage of a trial, to explain the impact that the crime has had on their lives. We also created the State Crime Victim Compensation Program and distributed millions of dollars in grants to local victim assistance programs. We created a "Victims' Bill of Rights"—eighteen specific rights that will give crime victims the information they need and the voice they deserve. The criminal justice process begins by giving victims or their families the right to be notified when an arrest is made, and it keeps them informed of each step along the way: when decisions are to be made about bail or bond, when court proceedings are scheduled and conducted, when any appeals are made, and finally, when release is being considered and made. Throughout the process, victims and their families have the opportunity to make their feelings known.

They have the right to tell the district attorney what they think about bail or bond release. This includes the right of input into plea or sentence negotiations, decisions about the defendant's participation in pre- or post-trial diversion programs, and decisions about parole. We also established a state-of-the-art automated calling center for registered victims of all kinds of crimes. It is called VINE, or Victim Information and Notification Everyday. Whenever an offender is released, the system will automatically contact all the registered victims of that inmate. It works in the other direction, too. Any registered victim can call in at any time from any phone and get a status report on their offender. These are the kind of things I would like to see nationwide and why I am a cosponsor of an amendment to the U.S. Constitution to protect the rights of crime victims.

Some may ask why take the dramatic step of an amendment to the Constitution? I answer: because criminals have more than two-dozen rights under the Constitution and crime victims have zero. A little one-sided, wouldn't you say?

Domestic violence is an undercurrent that only erupts into public view when it reaches devastating proportions. But it occurs in as many as one of every four American families. And it's tangled up in the intense emotions of the closest of all personal relationships. That makes it hard to address and prevent.

So, as governor, I added a staff person in each of the sixteen regions of the Georgia Bureau of Investigation with the sole responsibility for dealing with domestic violence. These agents were especially trained to handle all aspects of spouse, child, and elder abuse cases, including methods of questioning victims, witnesses, and the accused. Ninety-eight percent of child abductions are committed by mothers and fathers in connection with child custody fights, but it is the other 2 percent that recently has captured the attention of the media and generated tremendous publicity. It led to the Amber Alert System, which is a critical missing child response program that utilizes the resources of law enforcement and media to notify the public when children are kidnapped by predators. Law enforcement activates an Amber Alert by notifying broadcast media with relevant information. Once they receive the Amber Alert, the media interrupts regularly scheduled programming to notify the public that a child has been kidnapped.

I wish we could generate that kind of support to monitor and apprehend child molesters, the lowest of all criminals. These predators can never be rehabilitated and the hodgepodge of federal and state laws, along with the lack of close supervision, is a disgrace that must be remedied. I believe all convicted child molesters should have a microchip tracer implanted in his body when released from prison (the overwhelming percentage are males) so that his location can be pinpointed. Technology can pinpoint the location within seventy-five feet.

The sentence of "life in prison" has long been one of the biggest frauds in our judicial system. The so-called "life-sentence" actually amounts to eleven to thirteen years behind bars, in some states even fewer. Victims and their families deserve better than this; justice demands better than this. That is why I created in Georgia the nation's only two strikes law for violent felonies. That's right, two, not three like the Feds have. Three strikes is for baseball, not for those who commit violent crimes. For them it should be a second chance, but no more. The way it has worked since 1995 in Georgia, is that those who are convicted for the second time for murder, armed robbery, kidnapping, aggravated child molestation, rape, aggravated sodomy, and aggravated sexual battery are gone for life, never to get out of a Georgia prison again. That's what should be done on the federal level for all violent crimes. Anything less is inadequate and sends the clear message that crime does pay.

I support the death sentence. I have always supported it. I believe it is a deterrent to certain kinds of crimes. It may not be a deterrent to the highly emotional homicides that occur within families, but where it is associated with the commission of other crimes like armed robbery, it is definitely a deterrent.

Our juvenile justice system is in bad shape, too. Those of us who are parents and grandparents understand that in a personal way. I have been watching with grave concern as the number of children living in poverty, as has the number of babies born to drug-addicted mothers, as has the number of school dropouts, as has the number of children who are either victims or perpetrators of violence has increased, and as has the number of youngsters entering our juvenile justice system.

We live in a time when a healthy economy, jobs, and prosperity increasingly depend on a well-adjusted, productive, literate workforce. Unfortunately, at the same time, the odds seem to be stacking up against our troubled youth as we struggle toward that end. Pick any young offender from any youth detention center and look in his file. You will find a litany of problems: poverty, substance abuse, difficulties at school, a troubled family. And you immediately wonder, where were we along the way in that kid's life? How did things get so far out of hand? How could we have done a better job of prevention? Often it comes back to the parents, who should bear some of the responsibility and, yes, some of the punishment. Time and time again, we see a juvenile living with some elderly grandparent while the mother and father are nowhere to be found. I believe those parents should be hunted down. They are an accomplice to whatever crime the juvenile committed and I believe each should be punished as an accomplice.

Back when our juvenile justice system was created, a juvenile delinquent was a youngster who stole hubcaps, shoplifted, ran away from home, or painted graffiti on public property. Judges basically had two alternatives: a regular Youth Development Center or probation. No one envisioned the kinds of problems we are facing today where young people commit some of the most vicious crimes.

I believe that regardless of the age of the criminal, society must be protected and when I was governor I changed the way Georgia deals with young offenders. Starting at age fourteen, teenagers who commit certain violent crimes can be tried as adults and receive adult sentences. Of course, they should serve those sentences in a special youth facility, separate from the youth whose offenses are less severe and also separate from hardened adult offenders.

One of the greatest tragedies of modern society is the carnage on our highways caused by drunk drivers. It is raw violence, often inflicting injury and death on innocent victims. One out of every three vehicle crashes involves alcohol or drugs. The damage and loss in these cases tend to be extremely violent, and driving under the influence causes more than a third of the injuries and deaths on our highways. During my administration, we lowered the legal blood alcohol level for drivers, strengthened the penalties for driving under the influence of alcohol or drugs.

It has been my privilege to work with one of the greatest organizations in this country, Mothers Against Drunk Driving (MADD). Everyone should have to attend a MADD candlelight vigil. They come bearing the scars and the grief of having lost a loved one to a drunk or drugged driver. One can only imagine the intensity of their pain. You realize that nothing you can say— nothing anyone can ever say—will bring back their loved ones. It breaks one's heart.

Crime went down in the 1990s for the first time in decades and the reason it went down is because the bad actors were removed from the streets and put behind bars with longer prison sentences. Also, the death penalty began to be used more frequently. The old adage "crime does not pay" is only true when the punishment exceeds the profits. I know the bleeding hearts within and without my party will jump all over me about these beliefs. Well, as Sergeant Joe Friday of *Dragnet* would say, "That's just the facts, ma'am."

A Culture of Greater Expectations

18

Here is a snapshot of what our schools must become: Public schools will have computers in every classroom. All students will be assigned laptops as if they were books. Criteria for measuring academic performance of public schools will be standardized and federal funds will no longer flow to failing schools.

Parents and students will be able to choose which public school to attend. Students will be grouped according to their ability level. Persistent troublemakers will be assigned to alternative schools. A national curriculum will be established and standardized national tests will measure the academic achievement of students.

These will be schools of the future because ultimately the public will demand them.

I also believe the public will come to see the advantages of smaller schools. In smaller schools the student's performance is usually superior to that of students in larger schools. It is easier to involve "at risk" students in activities that mitigate the effects of low esteem. Small schools do a better job of redressing the negative effects of race and poverty and narrowing the gap separating achievement levels between advantaged and disadvantaged youngsters. Numerous studies indicate that small schools experience less violence and disruptive behavior. Students are less likely to drop out.

There is no question this nation has been changing in ways that complicate attempts to improve public education. As society has grown more complex, so have its problems. Many of those problems have fallen to our schools to address. In an effort to reduce teen pregnancy and drug and alcohol consumption, we ask schools to teach sex and drug education in addition to the three R's.

We ask schools to teach conflict resolution and help troubled students counteract the negative effects of violence on television and in electronic games. We expect schools to counteract our historic tendency to discriminate against women and minorities and to raise students' comfort levels with diversity. As important as this social education is, I regret to say much of it is coming at the expense of academic skills rather than as a valuable addition.

I've grown weary of expecting "education experts" to rescue our public school system. Education experts are like economists—even if you tried to lay them end-to-end, they would still point in every conceivable direction. One of my biggest frustrations is the culture of the education bureaucracy and the "educrats" and the "facilitators" who inhabit it under the leaky umbrella of "reform."

I'm not talking about the teachers. I do not bash teachers. They belong to the world's most noble profession and most of them are underpaid.

In the play *A Man for All Seasons*, Sir Thomas More is confronted by an ambitious young man looking for the way to fortune and fame. More advises him to become a teacher. "A teacher?" questions the incredulous young man. "Why? And if I were good, who would know?" More says, "Your pupils, your friends, God—not a bad public, that."

He was right; it wasn't a bad public in those days and it still isn't. But education's public has grown much broader since *A Man for All Seasons* was written. Fate has set the modern world on a course that places a heavy load of responsibility on teachers and schools.

When I was inaugurated as governor, the guest of honor, seated in the center of the front row, was Edna Herren, a teacher of mine at Young Harris College. She influenced my life in profound and pervasive ways that continue to have an impact on me after all these years. You can have all the national and state reform initiatives you want, but a good teacher will change your life forever. As a former and future teacher, I know that the heart of the education process is the relationship in the classroom of teacher, student, and subject matter. Public education will never improve unless we honor and respect that relationship more than we do now.

So, no, I'm not talking about teachers; I'm talking about those well-intentioned people who can sit in a conference room for hours at a time and speak to each other in a strange dialect that as far as I can see has no practical connection to anything that actually happens in a classroom. Then they walk out the door, and nothing changes. Still, they persist in wearing the badge reading "expert," believing firmly that nobody else understands what to do about education except them.

The complicated nature of education reform makes us vulnerable to what could be called "crowd-pleaser" activity, which means offering a simplistic solution to a popular issue in order to give the impression of reform. But school reform is a process, not an event.

That simplistic "crowd pleaser" mind-set tempts us to try to fix education by changing one or two things—then make a big deal about it. Unfortunately, everything else stays pretty much the same. Oh, we abolish social promotion. Or we give vouchers to students in low-performing schools so they can go elsewhere. We do a reading project in the early grades. We do a math project in the middle school. We put a computer lab in the high school. We argue over whether to fund smaller class size for the early grades or to use that money to improve the quality of our teachers.

Unfortunately, by themselves these piecemeal changes have been like panda matings. The expectations were high, but the results were disappointing.

Instead of arguing over which "one thing" by itself will transform education, we needed to step back and imagine a whole new picture. But before we can imagine, we must first forget old proprietary goals. The goal should not be just a new funding source. The goal is not even a particular project, although that is what the money funds. The goal should be to change the whole culture and climate of the school. Again, it is what I call a "culture of greater expectations."

We have known the basics of reform for years. We know that you have to reach kids and their families early, before the traditional start of structured education. We know we have to bring parents to school and involve them early, when the attachment between parent and child is still close. We know the most important factor in student performance and academic success is the effectiveness of the teaching in the classroom. We also know that you can further heighten student success in the early years by having teams of teachers who stick with the same group of kids and parents for a couple of years. We know that you need small class size, especially in the early years. That you have to have social service connections and coordination for kids who are at risk. We also know that you need support mechanisms for kids who are either gifted or slow learners.

We know all that. But if education reform is going to really work, we have to go a step farther. We also have to *evaluate* those models. You would think that educators by definition would have their eye on evaluation, on giving grades. They don't. For too many years, educational progress has been measured by listing programs and counting noses. If the programs exist and the kids show up, too many educators consider the job done. For years we thought a school was doing a great job if it followed all the rules and filled out all the paperwork on time. Student achievement had little to do with it. Research tells us that kids remember 10 percent of what they hear, 20 percent of what they see, 40 percent of what they discuss, and 90 percent of what they do. Yet we still stand the teacher up in front of rows of desks and assume that if the kids are quiet while the teacher's talking, they must be learning.

We must become more results-oriented. We need to be involved in a constant process of discovery, of identifying what works and what doesn't. We have to consistently ditch what doesn't work and redirect our resources to what does.

Comprehensive reform at the school level also raises that age-old administrative dilemma of top-down versus bottom-up governance.

Do we conclude that there is one right way to do education, and what we need to do is discover it and clone it so that every class-room and every school will be a cookie-cutter model of the same ideal? Or do we recognize that the essence of education is in the dynamic relationship of teachers and students with subject matter, and individual schools ought to have the freedom to develop that relationship in their own way?

In the past, we have erred on the side of top-down reform and top-down control. Professional "educrats" in the state department of education or the central office of the school system made deci-sions, then principals and teachers have been dispatched like foot soldiers to carry out orders.

Schools and classroom teachers have had little discretion over how they do their jobs, and they were seldom held accountable for their performance. Bad teachers were rarely fired, good teachers rarely rewarded.

Think about private schools for a minute. How do they do it? They know who their constituency is and they are accountable to it. They know what parents expect for that $20,000, and they deliver it. They set high performance standards and create a culture that meets those greater expectations.

Now think about public schools. When parents and taxpayers are unhappy with public schools, superintendents are sometimes fired and school board members sometimes lose elections. But those who actually make most of the decisions are insulated from the parents and the taxpayers inside the education bureaucracy, safe in their cocoon, from public pressure and accountability.

The challenge for the twenty-first century is to find the middle ground, where we have a common set of high standards and expectations for student achievement and performance, but then we allow schools freedom and individuality in deciding how to produce those results.

When education is run from the top down, decisions are made by people far removed from the students, who are the whole point of education, both the consumers of this service and the product of the process. Decisions tend to serve the internal convenience of the bureaucracy, rather than responding to the needs of the students.

No child was ever educated in the governor's office or the state department or even in the county school offices. Children are educated in schools and communities, not in bureaucracies, and it is from the teachers, parents, and business leaders that change must spring.

Schools must belong to their communities, not to government. If parents, businesses, volunteers do not have the opportunity to participate and contribute in meaningful ways . . . if they do not have a sense that the school will be accountable to them, then they will see no point in being involved.

Here is something so obvious it is ignored. Schools need to honor academic achievement at the same level as athletic achievement. I've been a jock, I've strutted around with a school letter on my jacket, and I've coached and taught many students who did the same. They were great kids; it is a badge of recognition, it makes one stand out. Schools should do at least the same for the top 5 percent of students in academic achievement. There should be tough interscholastic competition with a lot of publicity and award ceremonies. Just as in sports, there should be winners, losers, and runners-up.

The costs would be negligible, the social status significant. The leaders in some schools are so hare brained they won't even name a valedictorian because they don't want other students to feel badly. That's a disgrace and a detriment to teaching those kids how it is going to be in the real world. "Facilitators" do this kind of stuff, and I hate this therapeutic nonsense about everybody has to feel good. Show me a school or school system that emphasizes *how* children should learn rather than *what* they should learn and has "facilitators" instead of teachers, and I'll show you a failing system.

I also believe we should strike hard at the school-age drug culture. At seventy-one years of age, and having seen the drug culture from its beginning until now at various levels of the criminal justice system and the school system, I have concluded that while we will never stop drug use in our society as a whole, the least we can do is to make an all-out attempt to stop it among our youth.

Beginning in middle school and continuing through high school, we should periodically test students for drugs and the federal government should use part of those millions of dollars used in fighting drugs to pay for it. Drug users should be transferred to an alternative school that will offer rehabilitative services. This is the best way to get at it. Now, the ACLU crowd would climb all over it, but I believe it is legally defensible. This would stop drug trafficking in school and on school grounds. It might even keep that adolescent from becoming an adult drug user later on. If, and when, the student has been judged to be rehabilitated, he may reenter the regular school system for one more chance.

We didn't create a big state bureaucracy with Georgia's pre-K program, just a small office that mostly coordinates. We have clear state standards and expectations. But within the framework of those standards, each local pre-kindergarten program makes its own decisions. Each local program was designed by a team from its community to make the best possible use of their particular resources to meet their particular needs. Some pre-K programs are housed in public schools; others are private nonprofit centers in their own buildings or even in the education wing of a church. Some of them take a child-driven approach like Montessori; others use a more structured academic curriculum. All of them take a holistic approach not only to four-year-olds but also to their families. Every local pre-K has a family resource coordinator who makes sure the families in the program get the services they need. But the content of those services varies from place to place.

We began to evaluate the program the minute we started it. We asked the Department of Early Childhood Education at Georgia State University to conduct a three-year longitudinal study that followed the very first pre-kindergarten class through first grade. We compared them to their peers who had not attended pre-K, and we polled parents and teachers on their experience with the program.

The pre-K kids not only outperformed their peers in kindergarten and first grade, they also had lower rates of absenteeism and higher levels of parental involvement. This year another study showed the same positive results. We have also launched a twelve-year longitudinal study that will follow a large group of pre-K kids all the way into high school. I think the results of that study will be amazing. I hope to live to see it. To this day, I cannot understand why none of the other forty-nine states have done this.

Parents are not stupid. They can see that our economy is increasingly based on technology, and that the educational requirements of the average job keep going up. So parents want a good education for their children, because they know their children will have no chance for a good life without it.

For more than 200 years, education has been the magic that made the American Dream come true. Our schools have been the only public institution that guarantees every child the opportunity and possibility of upward mobility and full participation in our common civic culture.

Georgia has the only statewide pre-kindergarten program in the nation.

Democracy depends on each new generation growing up to be good workers, good parents, and good citizens. And with the exception of the home, the school is the best tool we have to achieve that. But that "tool" needs our help. Today, in too many places, especially in large cities, schools are owned by the unions and there are too many textbook publishers who sell their politically correct drivel in big, heavy, ultra-expensive textbooks that not only warp young minds but, when packed together in those got-to-have book bags, warp young spines as well. Only your local elected school board can do something about it. Your vote holds the key to that.

THE HIGHER CALLING OF HIGHER EDUCATION

19

A college education should be more than an item of currency to be traded on the job market. To view it solely as an economic asset is to devalue it. If that happens, it is no longer higher education, but merely vocational training. Higher education has the higher calling of educating historically literate citizens to be culturally tolerant, ethical, independent of thought yet mindful of community, and fully prepared to lead this nation in a century in which economic prosperity must be balanced with environmental sustainability and social equity.

It can be done. American history is on our side. Our elected leaders have always made education an over-riding priority. We have steadfastly refused to allow a variety of crises to distract us. Ironically, unsettled times, like those today, have often given us the push we needed to improve and expand education.

Two years before George Washington was inaugurated, the Continental Congress passed a law requiring every new township to set aside land for a public school. Even as the Civil War swirled around President Lincoln and our nation's Capitol was often in peril, Lincoln signed the Morrill Act, creating a system of land-grant colleges. In the middle of World War I, Congress passed the Smith-Hughes Act that established a new system of vocational education. With World War II raging on two fronts, Congress passed the Montgomery GI Bill, assuring returning veterans the chance of an education and changing the face of American society. When the Russians beat us into space with Sputnik, we strengthened math and science education. And we felt vindicated when we put a man on the moon.

We are the inheritors of those traditions. Today, we face outbreaks of violence that represent ongoing crises. But while war and rumor of war captures the headlines, we are also in the middle of one of the greatest economic and social shifts in world history. A great challenge of higher education is to move the nation toward a fuller understanding of what it means to be part of this global environment. Markets are already global; companies are increasingly international. Inevitably, business leaders are placing value on international experience and competence in the college graduates they hire. Presently, less than 10 percent of U.S. undergraduates study abroad. While we obviously must increase that percentage, the war with Iraq and the aftermath of 9/11 have made us more apprehensive about travel and study abroad, while at the same time making it even more necessary. Higher education must offer American students more opportunities to study outside our country, to become adept in other languages and cultures.

At the same time our economy grows globally sensitive, we also must adapt to the blurring speed of changing technology. There is more computer power in the Ford Taurus we drive to the supermarket than there was in the Apollo rocket that Neil Armstrong flew to the moon. Today, the combined forces of changing technology and global competition are bringing about a transformation that literally dwarfs the impact of the industrial revolution. These powerful forces are changing more than just our jobs. They are

changing the neighborhoods we live in. They are changing the institutions that shape our lives. They are changing our hopes and
dreams for the future.

Since the birth of this nation, the defining elements of American
society have been the idea of opportunity for all and the freedom to
seize it on behalf of our dreams. But for the first time in our history,
people aren't so sure about the reality of those dreams. It is a time of
profound insecurity for millions . . . a time in which the very plates
of the earth seem to be shifting under their feet.

Half of our population today is working harder than ever and
making less money. Half the people who lose their jobs today will
never find another job in which they will do as well.

The unemployment rate for high school dropouts is about twice
that of those with a high school diploma. For college graduates, it is
one-fourth that. So you can see, education doesn't matter just a
little. It doesn't even matter just a lot. It matters most of all.
Education is everything.

But while we used to view a high school education as the door
to opportunity, increasingly that is not even enough. A high school
diploma has lost its economic value. The median income of young
men ages twenty-five to thirty-four with a high school diploma has
fallen by $18,000 over the past two decades. More than half of newly
created jobs require education or training beyond high school. So, a
high school diploma has become, in effect, only a ticket to the post-
secondary education or training that will give you value in the job
market.

Over and over, I have argued, we must expect of students two
years beyond high school. I want the question to be not "whether,"
but "where" to go to college or technical school. I fought for
Georgia's HOPE Scholarship Program to open the doors of higher
education to all students who are willing to work hard and excel.
HOPE stands for Helping Outstanding Pupils Educationally. It is
based on merit, not means. You give something; you get something.
That is one of life's greatest lessons. Every single student in the state

who graduates from a public or private high school with at least a B average is eligible for a HOPE scholarship. It is possible to go through four years of college in Georgia and never pay any tuition. No other state can say that. Since the beginning of this program ten years ago, more than 700,000 students have benefited from it at a cost of $2 billion.

With much fanfare, in 1997 the president proposed and Congress created a federal version of the HOPE Scholarship Program. I traveled on Air Force One with President Clinton when he announced it at Princeton University. Later I sat in the gallery behind the first lady when he told the nation about it in his State of the Union address. Not everyone was enthusiastic about the initiative. I remember Clinton's chief of staff, Leon Panetta, growling in my ear, "This thing better work." Unfortunately, it hasn't worked because the similarity ends with its name. It is not a scholarship and it is not based on merit.

The federal HOPE program is a $1,500 tax credit and initial experience indicates this approach has had limited success. It is limited because the use of tax credits leaves it to the student to wrestle with IRS instructions and regulations. Worse yet, the timing of the financial benefit does not coincide with tuition bills. Furthermore, educational institutions hate the burden of having to provide IRS with information on students who use the credit, including information they may not be in the habit of collecting, such as parents' Social Security numbers if the parent rather than the student takes the credit.

Under the traditional model of student aid, the federal government and institutions of higher education were partners. Colleges made firsthand assessments of student need, then put together customized aid packages that often combined several fund sources in complementary ways. But, by resorting to a tax credit, the federal government has cut higher education out of the process. Many colleges now simply assume that all students have the tax credit in hand, and raise tuition accordingly, which for all practical purposes negates the effect of the tax credit. A more useful approach to student aid might be to acknowledge that managing a modern, efficient, $60 billion student aid delivery system is beyond the capability of the federal Department of Education. We should create a management system that is equal to the task and decrease the enormous regulatory burden imposed by the department, a cost that unfortunately is passed on to the students.

Because of advances in technology, the new trend of distance education has emerged and presents an additional problem for the program. The circumstances of distance learners are often remarkably different from those of traditional students, and the application and implications of student aid in this new context must be thought out.

For example, how long does this aid to education continue? Technology is changing so fast you can't just go through college once and be done with it. The shelf life of a technical degree is now down to five years. Lifelong learning has become reality and it means colleges and technical institutions are going to have to adapt to the needs of growing numbers of older, non-traditional students. Today, five of every ten American college students are over the age of twenty-five. Two of those five are over age thirty-five, and the percentage of college students over thirty-five has more than doubled in the past two decades. In the period between 1995 and 2015, the number of undergraduates will have grown by 19 percent, and only 60 percent of the total college enrollment will be white students.

The older population's need for continuing education is an additional complication since only a small fraction of that potential market for higher education can conveniently make it to campus when class is in session. But technology today offers education on demand—anytime and anywhere you can boot up a computer. It also offers the opportunity for interactive electronic classes in which students can participate simultaneously from the U.S. East Coast where it is 8:00 p.m. and Singapore where it is 8:00 a.m.

What's more, the development of Internet-based education has lifted higher education out of the sole possession of traditional colleges and universities, and placed it on the field of open competition. Even as universities scramble to offer online courses, Internet education providers are popping up in the business community. They pay professors for their course content, then package it, market it, and collect tuition fees from students, all without involving a traditional college or university anywhere in the process. These forces are rapidly reshaping how higher education carries out its historic missions of teaching, research, and service.

Even as college students grow more divergent, they also will become more diverse. In the past, higher education's efforts at diversity have been driven by the dictates of affirmative action or a sense of moral responsibility. However, we are quickly reaching the point where diversity will be the only way to maintain college enrollments and provide business and industry with the educated workforce they need. Minorities are especially sparse in science, math, and engineering; this is a matter of growing concern because the wealth and power of the world are gravitating toward those fields, and the leaders of tomorrow will be those who can create, apply, and manage technology.

As distance learning increases we must not overlook the fact that the strong economy we enjoyed during the 1990s was the fruit of university-based research from the 1960s, 1970s, and 1980s.

I have heard it said that the strong economy of the 1990s was not due so much to Bill Clinton as it was to Nikita Khrushchev. When the Russians developed a hydrogen bomb and launched Sputnik in 1957, it escalated the space and arms race and resulted in the federal government investing more heavily in research. Most of the research was done in higher education. Ostensibly for defense, the research surge greatly stimulated the essential fields of physics, chemistry, and electrical, computing, and mechanical engineering. The spin-off effects of these huge investments made years ago continue to help drive our economy to this day. For example, today's semiconductors emerged from federally funded university research in quantum mechanics conducted as far back as World War II.

The United States spends more money than any other nation on research and development, more than $100 billion annually. However, it is important to note that the patterns of investment have changed over time.

Back in the early 1960s, the federal government was the source of two-thirds of the R & D investment and industry was the source of one-third. The two lines crossed around 1980, and have gotten farther apart ever since, with industry conducting almost 70 percent of the nation's research while the federal government now contributes less than 30 percent. There should be a better balance. They should all move forward together. Growth in federal research funding slowed over the past decade and practically ground to a halt when the president recommended a $1 billion cut in the fiscal 2000 budget.

University research advances the science and technology that strengthen the economy, create jobs, sustain the environment, improve our health, enhance our quality of life, and maintain our leadership amid increasing global competition. We need a strong three-way partnership among government, higher education, and the private corporate sector.

During the next decade, America's schools will look to higher education to produce a record 2.5 million new teachers to address enrollment growth, replace those who retire or leave the profession, and respond to the popular demands for smaller class size. To improve K-12 education, and the quality of its own future students, higher education must move its teacher colleges from the periphery to the center of its efforts, improve their quality, and expand recruitment efforts. It goes without saying that instructors' salaries must be improved.

As a nation, we spend $300 billion a year for K-12 public education. More specifically, the federal government spends $2 billion to subsidize colleges of education and another $8 billion for remedial math and reading, but less than $300 million for research on the teaching and learning process.

But our schools and colleges must do more than prepare a capable workforce. As critical as technology is to our economy, we must never mistake it for culture. The business of education is more than mere information. The business of education is to transfer knowledge of what is meaningful in life. Unlike information, knowledge cannot be poured into the minds of students like water into a glass. It takes great teachers and workers/students who are continually learning new things and integrating what they learn into a life dedicated as much to the public good as to personal gain. We have to remind ourselves that what we do in our colleges and universities is as essential to living as it is to earning. That is the higher calling of higher education.

THE VALUES GAP

20

Writers have gained attention for years by declaring some precious value to be dead. German philosopher Friedrich Nietzsche got a lot of attention back in the nineteenth century by proclaiming, "God is dead." I like the response someone had on the death of Nietzsche. It went like this:

GOD IS DEAD! (Signed, Nietzsche)
NIETZSCHE IS DEAD! (Signed, God)

In 1965, an Emory University professor in Atlanta got himself a lot of publicity by again declaring God dead. I don't know exactly how he took God's pulse, but *Time* was so impressed with this "atheist theologian," as he called himself, that they chose Easter season to run a cover story on the demise of God. The Reverend Billy Graham's response was, "God is not dead; I talked with him this morning."

According to some recent book titles, God's isn't the only life-long friend I've revered and depended on that has shown up on the obituary pages. According to the authors of these books, Common Sense has died, as have Character, Truth, Right and Wrong, and the West. I hope it is not true, for all of them have served me well. I grew up with them. They served with me in the Marine Corps. I have told my children and grandchildren about them. They have been good and constant companions and, often when I stray, they have a way of finding me and straightening me out.

I want to believe their deaths have been exaggerated, as Mark Twain once put it when a premature obituary ran on him. No, they may look a little sickly lately, but this optimist will refuse to believe common sense, truth and character, right and wrong, or our Western way of life are dead until I see the still, cold bodies. If they are dead, as a variety of authors claim, I know this, they didn't die natural deaths; they were too strong. It wouldn't take TV's Quincy or Patricia Cornwell's Kay Scarpetta to declare it death by homicide.

Phillip Howard's book *The Death of Common Sense* was so thought-provoking that I required all my department heads in Georgia state government to read it. Howard says common sense was murdered by statutes created by a Congress dominated by special interests, and the accomplices are the faceless bureaucrats conceiving endless regulations. I take it he thinks that the cause of death was suffocation.

Author James Davison Hunter, in *The Death of Character*, performed an autopsy on that wonderful value and blames death on modern psychologists, at least those with their fuzzy thinking and teaching that says it is just fine and dandy to go ahead and do whatever makes one feel good about oneself. They teach that strict moral judgments are harmful to one's mental health and causes great damage to the psyche of this country. Hunter maintains—and I concur wholeheartedly—that forcing commonality in the name of therapeutic benefits rather than in the name of a self-governing sense of community is lunacy. Therapeutic anarchy can be so messy.

The Death of Truth, edited by Dennis McCallum, is a collection of writings about postmodernism. One of the most startling prem-

Visiting with Billy Graham at the Georgia Governor's Mansion.

ises in this book is the belief that all views, no matter how outrageous, are equally valid and that such a thing as one single truth
does not really exist. Don't laugh. This nutty idea can be found in
the textbooks many of our students use. It can be found in educational texts and history, law, and health care books. This strange
postmodern notion is responsible for a lot of today's political
correctness nonsense.

Peggy Noonan, the former Reagan speechwriter, wrote that
reading this book is "like prying up an iron lid and being dazed by
the gases that emerge." To the editor's credit, he does point out that
this movement should not be taken lightly and poses a real threat to
our culture and the church.

Pat Buchanan took it upon himself to deliver the eulogy for
what we regularly call "our way of life" in his book *Death of the West*.
According to Pat, who is so pessimistic he looks both ways before
crossing a one-way street, the West is going to hell in a taco basket.

He laments our apathy and inefficiency in assimilating immigrants. He rants about the myriad problems caused by these newcomers who don't carry the same aspirations and values exemplified by the wave of immigrants who helped form the backbone of America. I don't share Buchanan's pessimism, but I do share his concern. We had better give some serious thought about what is happening with immigration. We do need a better policy and we need it now, as I said in an earlier chapter. There are over 10 million illegal aliens in the country and the politics of dealing with them, the Hispanics especially, is so fraught with political consequences that no one on the political stage wants to touch it . . . except Pat.

Of all the autopsy reports I've read, none disturbed me more than *The Death of Right and Wrong.* I must admit I had never heard of the author, Tammy Bruce, until I came across this book. I don't know exactly what I expected from a self-proclaimed Los Angeles lesbian feminist, but it was certainly not anything like this. She takes us into a world that even this not-too-innocent seen-it-all found shocking. Her chapter on gangster rap is worth the price of the book. Every parent and teacher and public official should read it. Talk about a cesspool of depravity that so many of our youngsters— regardless of race—are swimming in and the fact that so many Americans do not even know about it is scary.

Now, I was not born under a cabbage leaf, and, as one might expect from an old Marine sergeant, my mouth ain't no prayer book. I can scorch one's tender ears with the best or worst of them. So it's not the profanity that bothers me; I can shed that like water off a duck's back. It's the sick, evil, and depraved thoughts that are expressed over and over again—thoughts too horrible to contemplate. Sadistic. Violent. Brutal. Sexual. Nasty. The pleasure of inflicting pain and mayhem on others. Against women ("bitches"). Against policemen ("pigs"). Against whites ("punk asses"). Against African-Americans ("trigger-happy niggas"). "Shoot ya in a minute"-type lyrics. Beating, thumping, pumping, pounding over and over hypnotically into some child's brain. I cannot imagine any parent allowing that to go on in their kid's bedroom. But it does in houses on every block in every city in this country. Too many parents try *not* to hear it. They go out of their way not to hear it. They go out of their way to be out of the way, and far too often, there is no parent even around. Twice in recent months I've seen a grieving parent on television explaining that their child had "just snapped." And we wonder why? There also is the parent who wants to be their child's best friend instead of being a parent and accepting the responsibility that goes with that honorable title. But worst of all are the multimillion-dollar recording moguls who distribute this dangerous and degrading filth in mainstream outlets. They should be horsewhipped.

Bruce maintains that the scandal within the Catholic Church has proved the Boy Scouts were right in prohibiting homosexual males from holding positions of "trust and authority" within the organization. But because of the highly effective gay public relations, the Boy Scouts have taken a beating on this decision. A number of organizations, not wishing to appear "politically incorrect," have withheld financial support. This includes many chapters of the United Way. A *Washington Post* article in August 2002 reported that a recent survey of 1,200 priests showed more than half said there was a "homosexual subculture" in their diocese or seminary. It is especially prevalent in seminary and doesn't have so much to do with pedophilia, which is defined as sexual contact with children twelve years old and under, as it does with adolescents. The magnitude of this problem even with all the publicity it has generated is still understated and only the Church itself can clean it up.

Despite all these books written about the deaths of key values, I have to believe there is a pulse left, faint as it may be. In fact, to put it in purely political terms, 25 percent of Americans are "value voters," and they always make the difference in a candidate winning or losing. Always! Later in this book I will argue that both Carter and Clinton got the Democratic Party nomination and won the presidency because their campaigns strongly emphasized, in varying ways, values.

What is a value? Why should it matter? Like that famous statement on obscenity, I may not be able to define it, but I know it when I see it—and so do one out of four American voters. They are not organized like some of the rich special interests in Washington, but the influence of these values voters is the most powerful of any segment of America. That is especially true in those red states that George W. Bush carried in 2000 and that the Democrats need to crack and the Republicans need to hold.

One shouldn't think of a value voter as someone totally rigid and unmovable from the extreme edges of ideology. For you see, the millions who have what they consider "the right values" do not expect a candidate to completely accept all of them. But, and this is the key, neither will they accept anyone spitting on what they grew up with and learned at their mother's knee. It is political suicide to give even the slightest hint that one is intolerant of their values. There is a big difference between disagreement and disdain. Value voters feel they have been used and are especially suspicious of Democratic candidates. They know that extreme liberal groups have come to dominate what was once, but is no longer, the party of Jefferson and Jackson.

As a teacher, coach, parent, grandparent, and great-grandparent, I've watched a lot of kids grow up. I can't help but worry about how today's youngsters, especially males, are going to survive their trip over what I call "Fools Hill." It's a trip common to all. Maybe it's the raging hormones or the way the brain is developing, but whatever it is, the only way parents can prepare their children for that inevitable journey is to emphasize substantive values.

The time it takes to get over Fools Hill varies. Sometimes it starts as early as thirteen or as late as twenty, but as sure as the sun rises each morning, that journey will be taken. And it can be rocky. It can be heartbreaking. That is why teaching values at an earlier age, before children begin that trip, is so important. The better they are taught before the journey, the more likely they will return with their values in tact. One other thing surely you know. A child pays very little attention to what you say to him, especially as the teen years approach. Words mean absolutely nothing, no matter how sincere or forceful you may be. Children do not do what they are told. They do as their parents do. Drinkers produce drinkers, bigots produce bigots, liars produce liars, junk food eaters produce junk food eaters.

Today's parents give in too easily to the pressures exerted by their children. Loving and well-meaning parents are so intent on giving their children what they didn't have when they were growing up that they have failed to give them what they did have: a sense of place, a sense of family, a code of conduct, a set of values. So, today both parents work so sixteen-year-old Junior can have a nice car to drive to school just like the other kids whose parents are doing the same thing.

Does having a car harm that teenager? Not unless he or she has one of the terrible accidents we read about almost daily. In my opinion, the damage comes if that kid gets that car without paying for it. Something for nothing, or almost nothing, is a terrible thing to give an adolescent. The lesson should always be, you give something and, then and only then, you get something.

You know from earlier chapters how much emphasis I place on early development of learning. I feel the same way about the establishment of values while the brain is still so receptive to stimuli. We have to understand, for example, that when a young person views imaginary violence it affects that child physically in the same way that viewing real violence does. This is true regardless of socioeconomic status or intellectual ability.

A nationwide study found that American children between eight and eighteen years of age spend six hours and forty-three minutes of every day exposed to media. When media were used simultaneously, like surfing the Internet while listening to music, the total rose to seven hours and fifty-seven minutes. That is more time than anything else they do except sleep. In the year 2000, a consensus statement by major health associations called violence in the media a public health emergency. Their research indicated a definite connection between that violence and aggressive behavior.

By the time an adolescent finishes high school he will have seen 100,000 assaults and 30,000 murders. These scenes do not pass harmlessly through a young person's brain. They are stored away and are easily recalled, producing long-time effects whenever the amygdala, an organ in the area of the mind that senses danger and prepares the body for fight or flight, activates in response to a threat. It causes a person to automatically respond like Arnold, Sly, or Clint would as the motor cortex kicks in and controls that person's spontaneous physical movement. Dr. John Murray of Kansas State University, an expert on neurological research, points out an even more volatile combination when sex is added to the cauldron of violence, both ingredients readily available via media.

As bad as some of our television and movies are they pale in comparison to video games. One of the most popular is *Grand Theft Auto III*, which links violence and sex and rewards players for degrading and killing women.

For anyone who doubts the dangers I've mentioned, I ask you to try to get children to sit still as they watch the Ninja Turtles or Power Rangers on TV. I promise that sooner rather than later, they will begin to push and shove and hit and wrestle and kickbox just like what they are watching. A generation ago it was reacting to the violence of the Three Stooges. Today, it is more graphic, more bloody, more brutal, and more sexual. So, my question is, what happens to our next generation? We should be concerned that they will have values geared toward the use of aggression to resolve personal conflicts, and they will be desensitized to violence.

In another of my books, *Corps Values*, I listed twelve values that were explained to me during my three months of boot camp. They were Neatness, Punctuality, Brotherhood, Persistence, Pride, Respect, Shame, Responsibility, Achievement, Courage, Discipline, and Loyalty. I devoted a short chapter to each. Some of these were qualities my mother, church, and school had already taught me. I believe that more of our citizens must learn them. I also believe these values can be taught to individuals or groups without infringing on a person's rights and beliefs.

Out of those values, I received the most criticism on Shame. Psychobabble from well-meaning, overeducated "professionals" who inhabit a rarified stratosphere above the real world ran amok in condemnation of this Neanderthal. But their tears and wringing of hands did not change my thinking; it strengthened it. What so many today do not understand is that humiliation can teach. Yes, I believe in corporal punishment, Dr. Spock's tender and permissive teaching to the contrary. My mother's rule was that if I got a whipping in school, another one was waiting for me when I got home.

Accepting the consequences of one's actions is one of life's most important lessons and when one chooses wrong over right and gets caught, that person should feel shame. If one doesn't, then what is one's motivation to do differently the next time? He'll just continue to repeat his mistakes. It's called recidivism in our criminal justice system.

When I was governor, I wanted to humiliate deadbeat dads and hoped it would produce enough shame to change them. I ordered "wanted" posters put up all over the state for dads who had skipped out on their children. Some permissive social workers complained, but Georgia became one of the leading states in the nation in the collection of child-support payments. I also wanted to put a photo in the newspapers of those poor creatures convicted three times of driving under the influence. Newspaper publishers did not want to do it.

I call this chapter "The Values Gap" for two reasons. One, it means about the same thing as "divide," a wide difference in character and attitude. It also has another meaning for this old mountaineer. A gap is a low place in a ridge, a pass where one can see what's on the other side of the mountain. It is a way through.

Just like Daniel Boone passed through Cumberland Gap and opened up a new frontier, so America can pass through the Values Gap and discover something about our fellow countrymen we haven't known. An in doing so, we may even discover something about ourselves.

When I reached my seventieth birthday in 2002, each of my four grandchildren gave me a present. I gave them this in return: "Some Lessons Learned by Seventy."

1. Don't be afraid to fail while going after something you really, really want. You will always learn from it. NEVER GIVE UP. Persistence will overcome everything else. I guarantee it.

2. If you listen more than you talk, you will not only learn more, but people will think you're smarter, not dumber, than you really are.

3. Take what you want. Take it and pay for it. You can have whatever you want but it's going to cost you in some way—something. For every action there is a consequence—always! It may be a good consequence or a bad one, but it will come just as sure as night follows the day.

4. Use frequently but sincerely the words "I'm sorry," "Thank you," and "I love you."

5. Being on time will be noted and will impress people. Being late is a rude thing to do. It says to the other people, "My time is more important than your time." A person who is always late is a selfish person. Mark it down.

6. Being mentally tough will help you more in life than being physically tough. They don't always go together.

7. People don't like to be around whiners. Don't be one. Ask yourself from time to time, "Am I whining too much?" Blaming others for your own misfortune is the same thing and just as bad.

8. Notice and appreciate what makes your heart leap up. Maybe it's a song or a poem or a movie or an event or location. Maybe it's

seeing, hearing, or reading something special. If nothing does this for you, examine your life because something is missing. Man does not live by bread alone.

9. Search for your own special niche. This may take years to find although often it occurs early in life. There is something out there that you can do better or easier than most other people can. You just seem to have a knack or talent for it. Find it. It's there. And when you do, others will beat a path to your door to get you to do it for them. It may bring you fame, fortune, or happiness. Keep in mind that there are also things you simply can't do very well, but there are others who can. If you're lucky, you'll marry one.

10. From time to time, make yourself do something you don't really want to do. It will make you stronger.

11. Family and home are very, very important. Honor them. One should know where one comes from and who worked or sacrificed to get us where we are. Having a sense of family and having a sense of place is going to be increasingly hard to have in this modern, fast-moving, ever-changing world in which you will live, but if you can have it, it will bring you much comfort and stability.

12. Keep a good sense of humor and laugh at yourself more than you do at others.

ONWARD, FREEDOM'S SOLDIERS

21

Good and evil take many forms and fight many battles with each other. Throughout recorded history, that struggle has too often taken the form of war between tyranny and freedom. We are forced to make a choice between the two. It always exacts a terrible toll, but thankfully it often results in the most glorious of payoffs when freedom wins.

It was true as far back as 490 B.C. The citizen-soldiers of Athens, Greece, turned back on the Plain of Marathon a Persian army three times as big and much better equipped. A man named Pheidippides ran the twenty-six miles back to Athens with the news of this great victory. Marathoners the world over still run that distance. But more than setting forever the distance of this grueling race, the far greater significance of this battle was that free men defeated the slaves and the king's hired soldiers.

This victory led the way to Athenian democracy and all the good things that went with it . . . the equality of citizens, individual rights, trials by jury, and freedom of speech. Of Athens it can be said: it was the first government "of the people, by the people, and for the people."

The glorious payoff was true that April day in 1775 when the local militia of the American colonists stood up to the British Redcoats at Lexington and Concord and fired the shot heard round the world. Two weeks later George Washington took command of the Continental Congress against the tyranny of George III, after which came the solemn statement of the Declaration of Independence: "We mutually pledge to each other our lives, future and sacred honor."

The payoff was gloriously true in 1863 when Abraham Lincoln made his famous address at that Gettysburg ceremony where 7,000 men had died and their bodies lay rotting for months after the battle. President Lincoln's few words explained better than anyone else ever has what the Civil War was all about: the test of whether "a new nation conceived in liberty . . . can long endure."

It was true—and eventually very personal—in 1917 when within a few months more than nine million Americans volunteered to fight the Germans in World War I and later turned the tide from stalemate and possible defeat into an Allied victory on the Western Front. My father was among them. I remember wearing his coat with the sergeant stripes when I was so young it dragged on the floor and my arms did not extend more than halfway down its sleeves. I have a brass artillery shell casing my father brought home. I keep it on the mantle of my home in Young Harris. Life in the trenches of that war was cold and damp, and when it rained the trenches flooded. Snails crawled out of the walls; rats and lice were everywhere. But the "dough boys" persevered. They were men of integrity, courage, and principle. They were patriots and I am proud to be one's son.

The glorious payoff was true in late spring 1940, because of a single strong voice. The voice rose in opposition to Adolf Hitler, as evil a man as ever lived. Hitler had just about extinguished freedom in all of Europe. As the clouds of war threatened to rain down on

England, Winston Churchill warned against the dangers of appeasement, pleaded that this evildoer must be stopped and destroyed.
Finally, in desperation, Great Britain turned to Churchill as its
prime minister and with stirring oratory and unflinching courage
he led them out from under the heel of Hitler.

I had come to believe that unless America found its own version
of Winston Churchill that the same spirit of appeasement, the same
kind of softness and self-indulgence would turn my country into a
modern version of a land cowering before the world's mad bullies. I
thought the signs evident in the American people and our leaders. I
thought our will as a country was vanishing. I was disgusted when
we did nothing after terrorists attacked the World Trade Center in
1993, killing six and injuring more than 1,000 Americans. I was
amazed in 1996 when sixteen U.S. servicemen were killed in the
bombing of the Khobar Towers and we still did nothing. When our
embassies in Tanzania and Nairobi were attacked in 1998, killing
263 people, our only response was to fire a few missiles on an empty
terrorist camp. It was a wimpy response so totally inadequate that,
as an American, I was ashamed.

Then came September 11, 2001, "the worst day in our history,"
as David McCullough has called it.

The next day after a sleepless night, I went to the floor of the
Senate and said:

> The victims and their loved ones of this horrible act of war should
> be in our prayers. The perpetrator and those who give them safe
> haven should be in our bombsights.
>
> After Pearl Harbor, a Japanese remarked that the "sleeping
> giant has been awakened." I pray that the sleeping giant has again
> been awakened. We've got to change the way we do things. For too
> long when terrorist attacks have happened, it seems America's
> first interest has been to please our friends, and then, if permitted,
> punish our enemies.

After yesterday and from here on out that must be reversed. America's first interest must be to punish our enemies, then, if possible, please our friends.

Our response should not only be swift, it must be sustained. As I said yesterday, our will as a country has been tested. Too often in the past, terrorist attacks have not been answered as forcefully as they should have. There's been indignation, even outrage. There's been wringing of hands and sad talk. We've shaken our collective heads in dismay, sighed over our cocktails, then went home, ate dinner, and went to bed, feeling safe and secure that it's not going to happen here. That it's not going to happen to us. Well, it happened to us. It has happened here. Our world has been turned upside down. It'll never be the same again. And it shouldn't.

We must strike the viper's nest, even if he's not there. We know that the Taliban and the government of Afghanistan has nurtured Osama bin Laden for years. This diabolical plot was probably hatched there. Certainly similar plots have been—and it's time for us to respond.

I say, bomb the hell out of them. If there's collateral damage, so be it. They certainly found our civilians to be expendable.

I got a lot of criticism for that statement, especially from some liberal press folks. But, in the months after I said we should "bomb the hell out of them," that's exactly what our military did in Afghanistan and two years later in Iraq.

A few days later, I traveled with most of the senators to New York City and visited Ground Zero. I saw its horror up close; I saw the grieving loved ones and the heroic workers going around the clock. I came back to Washington where the Senate was divided over creating a Department of Homeland Security. With the nation looking to us to beef up national security, Senate Democrats fought tooth and nail to block the new department solely to appease the federal employees union, which was ranting and raving and foaming at the mouth about job protection. It was an appalling

display, and I took to the Senate floor to tell the lessons of Churchill and Hitler.

> We are at a most serious time in the history of this land. Our country, our people are in mortal danger. And as I look at what is transpiring around me, this old history teacher cannot help but think about what the timid and indecisive Neville Chamberlain was told by a member of Parliament as he was dismissed as prime minister of Great Britain.
>
> "You have sat too long for the good that you have done," the member told him. I'm sorry to say it, but on this question of homeland security, I believe that most Americans think that this Senate has sat too long for the good that we have done.
>
> And as Chamberlain slunk away that historic day the crowd shouted after him, "Go, go, go." Then, you remember, Winston Churchill, who had been a voice in the wilderness warning for years about the threat of Hitler, became prime minister.

And in that famous first speech to Parliament in May 1940, he uttered those famous words, "I have nothing to offer but blood, tears, toil, and sweat."

Mr. President, what does this Senate, what do we have to offer in this time of crisis? How about a little bipartisanship perhaps? That's not too much to ask, is it, compared to blood, tears, toil, and sweat?

Because, as Churchill continued in that speech, "We have before us an ordeal of the most grievous kind." My Senate colleagues, we certainly have that today—an ordeal of the most grievous kind.

Churchill went on, "We have before us, many long months of struggle and of suffering. You ask what is our policy? I will say: It is to wage war, by sea, land, and air with all our might and with all the strength that God can give us: to wage war against a monstrous tyranny, never surpassed in the dark, lamentable catalogue of human crime. That is our policy. You ask what is our aim? I can answer in one word—victory—victory at all costs, victory in spite of all terror, however long and hard the road may be, for without victory there is no survival. Without victory, there is no survival."

And then Churchill said, "At this time I feel entitled to claim the aid of all, and I say Come, then let us go forward together with our united strength."

Then, Clement Attlee, the leader of the opposing Labor Party, joined with Churchill as his deputy prime minister and they worked together during the course of the war.

Why can't we have something like that around here now? Is it too much to ask when we are in a death struggle for the soul of mankind?

Unfortunately, the partisanship continued in the Senate. Vote after vote was taken and I remained the only Democrat supporting President Bush on Homeland Security. Fortunately, the president moved ahead with plans for a regime change in Iraq. I immediately gave him my full support and told a true story to my colleagues.

Mr. President, I have signed on as an original cosponsor of the Iraq resolution, and I'd like to tell you a story about why I think it is the right path to take.

A few weeks ago, we were doing some work on my back porch back home, tearing out a section of old stacked rocks, when all of a sudden I uncovered a nest of copperhead snakes.

Now, I'm not one to get alarmed at snakes. I know they perform some valuable functions, like eating rats.

And when I was a young lad, I kept snakes as pets. I had an indigo snake, a bull snake, a beautiful colored corn snake and many others. I must have had a dozen king snakes at one time or another. They make great pets and you only had to give them a mouse every thirty days.

I read all the books by Raymond C. Ditmars, who was the foremost herpetologist of the day. That is a person who is an expert on snakes.

For a while, I wanted to be a herpetologist, but the pull of being a big-league shortstop outran that childhood dream.

I reminisce this way to explain that snakes don't scare me like they do most people. And I guess the reason is that I know the difference between those snakes that are harmless and those that will kill you.

In fact, I bet I may be the only senator in this body who can look at the last three inches of a snake's tail and tell you whether it's poisonous or not. I can also tell the sex of a snake, but that's another story.

A copperhead will kill you. It could kill one of my dogs. It could kill one of my grandchildren. It could kill any one of my four great-grandchildren. They play all the time where I found those killers.

And you know, when I discovered these copperheads, I didn't call my wife Shirley for advice, like I do on most things. I didn't go before the city council. I didn't yell for help from my neighbors. I just took a hoe and knocked them in the head and killed them— dead as a doorknob.

I guess you could call it a unilateral action. Or preemptive.
Perhaps if you had been watching me you could have even called
it bellicose and reactive. I took their poisonous heads off because
they were a threat to me. And they were a threat to my home and
my family. They were a threat to all I hold dear. And isn't that
what this is all about?

Of all the speeches I've made over the years as governor and
senator, I think I received more positive reaction from this one. I
think it was because I expressed the frustration caused by the time-
consuming debate in the United Nations and how France and
Germany, after all we had done for them, turned their backs on us.

Like most Americans, I became highly agitated with the way
France behaved as we prepared to do battle with Saddam Hussein. I
muttered some choice words about them, the best of which was
"ingrate." Then, the long reach of history took over and I remembered it had not always been such. My home state of Georgia, the
youngest and most vulnerable of the original thirteen colonies, got
unforgettable help in the dark days of the Revolutionary War. Count
Charles-Henri d'Estaing, the dashing French naval commandant
who was a great admirer of George Washington, brought 4,500
Frenchmen and twenty-two ships to help in the siege of Savannah.
France's Pierre L'Enfant was wounded in Georgia and left for dead
but lived to later design Washington, D.C. Johann DeKalb, the son
of a Bohemian peasant and a very brave man in the French Secret
Service, also fought gallantly on behalf of the colonies. He was killed
in the Carolinas with nineteen wounds to his body. Georgia remembered him so favorably that they named a county after him.

But without question, the one who gave us the most help was
one of freedom's greatest soldiers, the Marquis de Lafayette, only
nineteen when he came to America to fight for our liberty.
Benjamin Franklin, our minister to France, had suggested he come
and at first, George Washington hardly knew what to do with the
redheaded teenager. But the general, always a good judge of char-

acter, gave him a commission and he turned out to be a brave and able leader who helped defeat the British at Yorktown.

Lafayette was from one of the richest families in France, but a love of liberty burned in that thin body. He wanted to help us gain our freedom so much he left his young wife and baby at his vast estate to come to this country and fight for its ideals. When France suffered its own revolution, Lafayette sent Washington a key to the Bastille, the terrible prison that the people had stormed. It still hangs in the hall at Mount Vernon.

Two counties and two cities in Georgia are named for him and a third city, LaGrange, was named for his farm in France. On the LaGrange Square is an impressive statute of this man, a soldier of freedom on two continents. So, I have to remember that there were once Frenchmen like Lafayette.

Our state's history is replete with stories of heroes in the pursuit of freedom. Our founder, James Edward Oglethorpe, understood from day one how important it was to have a strong military force. Oglethorpe successfully built a new colony on a piece of land that for 200 years had been in contention among the English, French, and Spanish, to say nothing of several Indian tribes. Georgia was an important buffer between his fellow English in Charleston and on up the Atlantic coast and the Spanish in what is today Florida. The Colony of Georgia was not even ten years old when Spanish troops marched northward in 1742, intent on expanding their territory.

The newly formed Georgia militia was the first line of defense against that expansion. At the Battle of Bloody Marsh on what is now called St. Simons Island, Oglethorpe and his little Georgia militia turned back the Spanish. It was not only a military victory of the moment, but also one of those defining events that take on greater significance in retrospect, since they shaped the course of history.

Had Oglethorpe not defeated the Spanish, they may very well have swept on northward, catching the colony of Carolina unprepared. No one knows where that story might have ended, but the

American South might be speaking Spanish were it not for Oglethorpe. And the United States may never have emerged as one of the great powers of the world.

Few of freedom's soldiers have understood the lessons of history as well as Winston Churchill, who not only was a brave and daring soldier and a great political leader, but also was a Nobel Prize-winning historian. Perhaps, then, in these times we should remember the question Churchill framed to the world when he made his famous Iron Curtain speech in Fulton, Missouri, at Westminster College in 1946.

He first reminded his audience that war and tyranny remain the great enemies of mankind. Then he asked these questions: "Do we not understand what war means to the ordinary person? Can you not grasp its horror?" For all the necessity of war, the old warrior said some very sensible and thought-provoking things on the other side of the coin, like "War used to be squalid and glorious, now it's just squalid."

The bluntness with which Churchill spoke about the looming threat of the Soviet Union in that speech did not go over well in many quarters. The American media did not want to hear that kind of talk. They called him a "war monger." Even the usually gutsy Harry Truman denied knowing in advance what was in the speech and even suggested Churchill should not have given it. But, today that line about war is worth remembering: "Do we not understand what war means to the ordinary person? Can we not grasp its horror?" Abraham Lincoln was just as realistic. "You don't fight war by blowing rose water through corn stalks," he said. These two men, each the greatest man of his century, knew the horrors of war. But they also knew that they are sometimes necessary, that there is more to civilization than just comfortable self-preservation, as too many think today. Soft-belly peaceniks believe war is politically pointless and that foreign policy is like so much fuzzy-feeling social work. I reject that. Sometimes a short war must be fought to prevent a longer war. Sometimes hundreds may die in order to save thousands. Sometimes the long view of history must be taken.

In my Senate office in the Dirksen Building in Washington, I have a 3'-x-5' painting of the raising of the flag at Iwo Jima. I had it behind my desk at the State Capitol in Atlanta when I was governor. To me, that image of six men raising an American flag on Mount Suribachi in one of the bloodiest battles ever fought is one of the world's most vivid symbols of the price of freedom. The photograph from which it was painted is the most reproduced in the history of photography.

Those flag raisers were very young men, just boys really, six of America's best from all corners of our country. That is another reason it holds so much significance. There was a coal miner's son from Pennsylvania, a farmer's son from Kentucky, a mill worker's son from New England, and another farmer's son from Wisconsin. One came out of the oil fields of Texas and one was a Pima Indian from the Gila Reservation in Arizona.

Three of those boys would never leave the island and would be buried in that black volcanic ash. One would leave on a stretcher, and the other two would come home to live miserable lives of drunkenness and despair. Only one would somehow be able to overcome that island and the event with any degree of peace of mind. He was a Navy corpsman, assigned to the Marines to help with their wounded and dying. His name was John Bradley, and in the year 2000, his son James wrote a memorable book, *Flags of Our Fathers*. The great historian Stephen Ambrose called it the best battle book he ever read. I recommend it highly.

As one looks at the painting or photograph, this image of courage and sacrifice, it is easy to miss what I consider to be one of the most important things about it. Bradley points this out. There are six boys in it but unless you look very closely, you see only five. Only the helping hand of one is visible. Most significantly, they are virtually faceless! Only a somewhat vague profile of one can be seen at all. If you are like most Americans who have looked at this famous scene time and time again over the past six decades, you may have missed that one important feature: one cannot really identify a single individual's face.

But isn't that really the way it has always been with most of freedom's soldiers—unknown and, all too often, unappreciated? They are those faceless, nameless "grunts" who fight our wars to keep us free.

While I speak of the wages of war, let me also make this clear: one does not have to wear a uniform or hold a public office to be one of freedom's soldiers. One does not have to carry a gun or brandish a sword. One does not even have to go through boot camp. One does not have to be a male. One only has to be armed with courage and love of liberty.

Rosa Parks was a soldier of freedom when she refused to move to the back of the bus in Montgomery. That young minister named King up at the Dexter Avenue Baptist Church took up the cause, and, with words sharper than any bayonet and deadlier than any bullet, slayed the evil of segregation and brought freedom to millions of people. Young John Lewis risked his life at the Edmund Pettis Bridge as he marched for liberty, just the same as those farmers had at the Concord Bridge.

Abigail Adams, Susan B. Anthony, Elizabeth Cody Stanton, Lucretia Mott, and Mary Wollstonecraft were all freedom's soldiers in their time fighting in the trenches and on the battlefields for women's liberty.

Some of freedom's soldiers used the pen instead of the sword. John Stuart Mill with his essay "On Liberty," and Thomas Paine in *Common Sense* provided inspiration to the freedom lovers who read their words.

But there are also times when the only solution is war, when, as that great hymn goes, we must "rise up and put our armor on." And what armor it is! High tech weapons and equipment, the likes of which no one could ever have imagined a few short years ago. So sophisticated and complicated that freedom's soldiers must now be trained in chemistry, biology, and electronics as well as traditional fighting skills.

America has the most highly trained and best-educated soldiers in all our glorious history. Yet, as the heroic rescue of Pfc. Jessica Lynch showed so clearly, they also understand and live by our warrior's most sacred promise, "Leave no soldier behind."

I admire the songwriter Kris Kristofferson. His words and music elevated country music to a new, inspiring level. But that line in "Me and Bobby McGee" about "freedom's just another word for nothing left to lose" has always disturbed me. I do not believe it. I reject it. It is not true. It was written in the late 1960s about the same time I recall seeing a news photograph of a protesting student in the days of the Vietnam War. He was carrying a sign with the words "Nothing is worth dying for." I remember thinking then, as I do so today, that if there is nothing worth dying for in our America, then there is truly nothing here worth living for, either.

I watched the war with Iraq with pride, but could not help marveling, "Where do we keep getting these young men and women? Where do they come from?" It's amazing that our country produces them when we consider how many young people on our college campuses and workplaces do not have this love of country and a willingness to die for it. Amnesia has either set in or there is total apathy about what has transpired in our history and the huge price that has been paid for freedom. The history of freedom should be a required course just as there once was on the history of Western civilization.

Hubris is best defined as "outrageous arrogance." And if you study the lessons of history, which, as I said, we don't anymore, you would find that hubris has time and time again brought down powerful civilizations. We are in grave danger of that happening today. There is no greater example of outrageous arrogance than in Hollywood, from those who live in a make-believe world and think they carry more influence than they do.

I am fed up with Hollywood weenies like Martin Sheen and Sean Penn making millions of dollars playing soldiers in films like *Apocalypse Now* and *Casualties of War* and then in real life giving the finger to those who really wear the uniform. To me, they are lower than a snake's belly, hypocrites at best, all gurgle and no guts. Rapper Ice-T is just as bad. This hypocrite got rich with his hit in the early 1990s called "Cop Killer" with the refrain "Die, Die, Die, Pig, Die! Fuck the police." And then he portrays a pony-tailed detective on the popular "Law and Order" television program. That's hubris. That's hypocrisy. That's a disgrace.

Someone once said that in the long course of world history, freedom has died in many ways. Freedom has died on the battlefield, freedom has died because of ignorance and greed, but the most ignoble death of all is when freedom dies in its sleep. It's time these so-called public figures wake up from that special place they go to dream their ridiculous fantasies. It's also time for a wake-up call in the U.S. House, where a few elected members, sworn to preserve and protect, visited the enemy and became unwitting toadies and tools for dictators and wanna-be Hitlers through their reluctance to make tough decisions. I saw it in the U.S. Senate where, almost casually, a few union jobs were put above the security of a nation in wrangling over homeland security.

But where you would not see it was in the Bush White House and at 10 Downing Street in London. For President Bush and Prime Minister Blair, like Lincoln and Churchill before them, understood that there is always the ongoing struggle between good and evil and one must have steel in one's spine to take a stand between the two. History will be especially kind to these two twenty-first-century soldiers of freedom.

HOW CARTER RAN AND WON—ONCE

I have followed the game of baseball since I was ten years old. I played it and even coached it three seasons at a junior college. So I'm going to use some of its terminology as we look at the last nine times the Democratic team has been to bat. Three times we got a hit. None of them were anything to brag about, but at least we got on base. Two times we grounded out and once the play at first was very close. Four out of nine times we struck out. We went down swinging and flailing at balls that were in the dirt or over our heads and it was not a pretty sight. It caused me to wonder what these players were doing in the major leagues.

The two groundouts were in 1968 when Humphrey lost to Nixon 301 to 191 and in 2002 when Gore was called out in the closest call in big league political history. The strikeout victims were McGovern in 1972, Carter in 1980, Mondale in 1984, and Dukakis in 1988. McGovern lost every state except Massachusetts; Carter suffered the worst defeat of any Democratic incumbent in history when he carried just six states. Four years later Mondale carried

With President Carter and President Clinton.

only his home state of Minnesota—barely. In 2000 Al Gore became the second Democratic candidate who couldn't even win his own state's vote.

So only Carter in 1976 and Clinton in 1992 and 1996 managed to get on base. Now, what they did after they became base runners I will leave for someone else to discuss. The point is these two Southern governors somehow managed to do what the others could not do: get elected. Frankly, the others embarrassed themselves and the party trying.

Now, as fate would have it, I knew both Carter and Clinton before and after they got those hits. I watched them in the minor leagues so to speak. I watched how they developed their swings, observed their desire quotient (high), marveled at how they studied the opposing pitchers, how some pitches they could hit better than others; how some they could knock over the fence. Both could do what all great hitters do, go with the pitch and hit to the opposite field. Neither pulled the ball to extreme left or right field. Both ran the bases with their spikes high and both would run over you. If this baseball lingo is going to far, let me return to English. I know them both well enough to know they would not like being compared to each other, but the similarities jump out at you.

First, and this is important, they were both Southern governors, and both suffered early career setbacks because they were considered too liberal. Both were raised by opinionated, free-spirited mothers. Both married strong women and take great stock in their opinions. Both have superior intellects, perhaps in the top five among all presidents. Both have a deep and abiding belief they were destined to do something great. Both have unbelievable stamina and drive. Both have large egos, can be mean-spirited and when threatened will not hesitate to turn negative. But both could also make you feel as if you were the only one in the room and they were concentrating on each syllable and great thought you uttered. Both are concerned how history will remember them and have great reluctance to step off its stage even if it means embarrassingly upstaging their predecessors. To their last gasp of breath, each will be working to shape and reshape how history remembers them.

They also had noticeable differences. Carter wanted to make all the decisions himself. Clinton needed staff around him all the time. Carter is highly disciplined. Clinton is not. Carter is most comfortable in a small group and most uncomfortable with a large crowd in a large hall. Clinton is most at ease in African-American churches and most uncomfortable on military bases. Carter is comfortable around farmers; Clinton is not. They both love the challenge of being around the intelligentsia and matching brains with them. Neither enjoys having to work things out with dumb, pesky legislators. They're beneath them and are flies to be swatted.

I had been a state senator for two years when Carter came to that body in 1963. He quickly impressed everyone with that smile, that first-class mind, and that relentless work ethic. He read every bill introduced in the Senate and the House and he wanted everyone to know he did. Some members who preferred the nightlife called him an overeducated fool with no common sense. He wasted little time in becoming a candidate for governor and, in 1966, finished third behind Lester Maddox, the arch-segregationist, and Ellis Arnall, the aging and progressive former governor of the 1940s.

Almost immediately after he lost, Carter started a nonstop campaign for another run in 1970, crisscrossing the state time and time again. He stayed in peoples' homes, shook over 600,000 hands, and made over 1,800 speeches. Nevertheless, one year prior to the primaries the polls showed him trailing former governor Carl Sanders 53 to 21 percent.

Carter refused to accept the odds; he did not intend to lose again. In his book *Why Not the Best* he tells of writing a memo to his campaign on the direction he believed they must go to defeat Sanders. Notations on his yellow legal pad included "Sanders more liberal . . . excluded George Wallace from coming to Georgia, pretty boy, nouveau rich."

Running basically as a rural Georgian, he began to call Sanders "Cufflinks Carl." For his billboards and brochures, he used the most ugly picture he could find of himself in work clothes to draw the contrast between him and the handsome former governor. One of his television ads showed a door to a country club with a voice saying, "This is the door to a exclusive country club where the big money boys play cards, drink cocktails, and raise money for their candidate—Carl Sanders. People like us are not invited. We're busy working for a living. That's why our votes are going to Jimmy Carter . . . our kind of man." Negative leaflets appeared like autumn leaves. One showed a photo of two African-American Atlanta Hawks basketball players pouring champagne over Sanders' head after a winning game. Another leaflet pointed out that Sanders had attended the funeral of Martin Luther King Jr. (Carter had not.)

Georgia's political campaigns have always been rough. The most recent one had the incumbent governor Roy Barnes pictured as a big rat named "King Roy." But it was much rougher in 1970. It worked. Carter won and a few months later, looked out over the crowd gathered for his inauguration and declared, "I say to you quite frankly the time for racial discrimination is over. No poor, weak, or black person should ever have to bear the burden of being deprived of the opportunity for an education, job, or simple justice." Shortly thereafter, *Time* put Carter on its cover as "the face of the New South."

Six months after he took office, I went to work for him as the executive director of Georgia's Democratic Party. My responsibility was to oversee putting the new so-called McGovern rules into effect. During the disastrous 1968 Democratic Convention in Chicago where protestors and Mayor Richard Daley's policemen clashed repeatedly on national television, a resolution was narrowly adopted to establish a reform commission "to create a more democratic procedure" for the selection of delegates. The long-standing process of leaving it up to the state parties that had nominated such winning candidates in the past as FDR and Truman was to be abolished. Senator George McGovern of South Dakota was named chairman of the committee. Its goal was to attract more women, minorities and youth. It was called, "participatory democracy" and the Party has not been the same since. In Georgia at a congressional district caucus, Charles Kirbo, the state Democratic Party chairman and Governor Carter's closest friend, was defeated by a female college student. But good Democrats like John Lewis and Julian Bond, among others, were chosen. It was not all bad.

As I survey the wreckage of that chaotic and historic 1972 convention held at Miami Beach, I think the lessons learned is that there's only a slight difference between extreme "participatory democracy" and anarchy. It also brought more female participation. One of my most enduring memories is that of the late New York congresswoman Bella Abzug. Loud, built like a linebacker with a big umbrella-like hat, she was a formidable presence. So were Gloria Steinem, Shirley MacLaine, and Shirley Chisholm. It was also where I got to work closely with John Lewis and Julian Bond. In fact, both

Julian and I got to speak for a few minutes at the convention. We had worked out a compromise on the seating of certain Georgia delegates for the convention to accept. Some may remember that Julian had been nominated for vice-president at the 1968 Chicago convention and then made an eloquent statement of regret since he was not old enough to hold the office. But to my way of thinking, the most worthwhile thing that came out of the whole wild week was that country singer/songwriter Tom T. Hall on his way back to Nashville from the convention had a moment of inspiration and wrote on the back of a vomit-bag in the plane one of his best songs, "Old Dogs, Children, and Watermelon Wine."

After that, my job would be to help the presidential nominee to do well in Georgia and help elect a new Democratic U.S. senator over Fletcher Thompson, whom we all knew would be a tough Republican opponent. Senator Richard Russell had died in January. Governor Carter appointed David Gambrell, an Atlanta lawyer, to the position. Republican Thompson was waiting to take him on. But there were a number of other Democrats who planned to challenge Gambrell in the Democratic primary. Among them were former Governor Ernest Vandiver and a little-known Middle Georgia state legislator named Sam Nunn.

As sort of a residual benefit of all this, I had the opportunity to meet, greet, and eat with the various presidential candidates coming to Georgia during this time. I enjoyed doing that, getting to know them and observing their talents up close. Little did I know until toward the end of the campaign, that the person studying them the closest, really taking their number, was Governor Carter. He frequently invited them to stay overnight at the Governor's Mansion where he could take a really close look. And as he compared himself to them, it became clear that he was smarter and could campaign circles around any of them.

Carter waited as late as possible before he settled on Senator Henry ("Scoop") Jackson and was selected to nominate him at the Miami convention. I was a Jackson delegate and was on the National

Platform Committee. Four years later Carter, himself, would wreck Jackson's chances by defeating him in the 1976 primary in Pennsylvania.

As the four years of the Carter administration in Georgia came to an end, he rewarded me with a safe seven-year appointment to the Pardon and Parole Board. Less than a year later I left it to run for lieutenant governor. Just as Carter had studied national contenders, I had been studying statewide candidates and knew deep down I could compete with them.

On December 12, 1974, Carter surprised everyone when he announced he was going to run for president. Even his mother, Miss Lillian, asked him, "You're running for president of what?" At that time, the conventional wisdom was that one needed a platform from which to run. Carter believed differently. Not having an office gave this Energizer Bunny all the time he needed to campaign everywhere. With his loyal band of Georgians, Hamilton Jordan, Jody Powell, Gerald Rafshoon, and Frank Moore, he began his amazing journey.

Here was a family man, a military man, a Naval Academy graduate, a peanut farmer, a businessman; you name it, he had done it. His Baptist background strongly worked in his favor. He said that he sensed "a moral hunger in the electorate" and as a born-again Christian, this Sunday school teacher fed on that hunger. "I'll never lie to you," he told America over and over. That went over well with the memories of the lying President Richard Nixon still hovering over the land.

"Brother Jimmy," as the Reverend M. L. ("Daddy") King Sr. called him, dominated the African-American vote in the primaries and later in the general election. At first, the labor leaders had a hard time accepting this Southerner because Georgia is a right-to-work state, which means that union membership is not a requirement for employment. Northerners, especially liberals, found the soft Southern accent foreign to their ears, some complaining that they could not understand him.

I have found out the hard way that there are people in this land who equate a Southern accent with stupidity. Raymond Strother, for decades one of the Democrat's premier media consultants, tells the story in his fascinating book *Falling Up* of being rejected in 1988 by the Dukakis campaign after an interview with his staff. To his credit, the candidate himself explained why. "It is just your accent. People up here equate the Southern accent with people who aren't as smart as they are. Those are mostly Harvard graduates, and they will never have confidence in you." Dukakis, a decent man, was just telling it like it was—and is.

If there was a single reason Carter got the nomination, it was because he was an outsider, but not a George Wallace. Every other Democrat represented the establishment. Scoop Jackson, Lloyd Bentsen, Sargent Shriver, Birch Bayh, and Fred Harris were all Beltway insiders, four of them U.S. senators. Over and over, Carter told audiences, "I owe nothing to special interest groups," and it resonated. It would in 2004 if anyone had the guts to say it.

Carter ran in thirty of thirty-one primaries and showed the kind of stamina no one ever had seen before. This was a man used to getting up before daylight and staying up without sleep for days at a time during the peanut drying season. A dozen years later, after the 1988 presidential race, Richard Ben Cramer would write his fascinating book *What It Takes*, telling of the unbelievable torture a candidate puts himself through during a presidential campaign. Carter invented that torture chamber in 1976 for all those who would come after him.

No candidate before him had ever shown the personal attention that he did to the Iowa caucus. After him, it became the thing to do, the way to run. He crisscrossed that state, staying in homes, washing his socks and underwear and hanging them in the bathroom, and always making up the bed in the morning. In the end, even with all the hard work and all the visits, he barely carried the Iowa caucuses. But he won and that was what was important.

The victory surprised everyone, most of all the folks back in Georgia. I was lieutenant governor and until this time was the only statewide elected official who openly supported our former governor. But then things began to change—everywhere. The "Peanut Brigade" had long before laid the groundwork in New Hampshire so the momentum from Iowa led to another victory in New Hampshire. Carter headed south to face George Wallace in Florida. This was the High Noon showdown because Wallace had won the state big in 1972. This time Carter cleaned his clock. I was with him the night of the primary in Florida and remember him coming barefooted to the room where Herb Green, Georgia UAW leader and good friend, and I were and we hugged him and basked in the euphoria. It continued in Illinois. Hubert Humphrey and Frank Church and Jerry Brown tried to stop him but they were too late. The nomination was his and the polls had him leading the incumbent President Jerry Ford by thirty points.

As I've said, the national labor leaders were very suspicious of Carter, but it helped when he chose their favorite, Senator Walter Mondale, as his running mate. It would always be a shaky alliance; they simply did not trust each other.

In the end it was the South that saved Carter in November. He carried every state in the Old Confederacy except Virginia. He also carried the border states of Kentucky, Maryland, and Missouri. These thirteen states provided 149 electoral votes, over half his winning total of 297. This was different and significant because Georgia and the South had voted Republican in two out of the last three elections and would in the next three elections.

Four years later, after double-digit inflation, waiting in lines to buy gas, and the endless ordeal of the hostages in Iran, Carter received the smallest vote in history of any Democratic incumbent. This Georgian, who had generated so much regional pride, saw his Southern base decimated. Only his native state stayed in the Democratic column. Some Southerners would say he forgot where he came from. Others would say it was the magic of Ronald Reagan.

I say it was because after campaigning as a new kind of Democrat, he governed too much like an old one. He tried to satisfy the ravenous appetites of those special interest groups, which will always kill you. He promised and delivered to the NEA a new Department of Education, and to the environmentalists a new Department of Energy. Unfortunately, that did him little good. They always want to know what you can do for them tomorrow.

Walter Mondale saw who had helped do Carter in. In 1984 he would grovel as no candidate had ever groveled to these groups, giving in to their every desire. They asked for it, they got it. It would lead to the Democratic Party's most ignoble defeat. Mondale carried his home state of Minnesota by less than 5,000 votes and lost the other 49.

I saw this up close. In fact, it splattered all over me. Jim Johnson, Mondale's main man, came down to Georgia and asked me to serve as state chairman for Mondale. Ovid Davis, a good friend and chief lobbyist for Coca-Cola, urged me to accept, but I was mostly persuaded by many of my Carter friends who said it was the least I could do for someone who had been so "loyal to Jimmy." So I ended up assuming that job and escorting the candidate around Georgia. Mrs. Mondale traveled through North Georgia with Shirley. We hosted a reception for her at our home in Young Harris. I have to say, politics aside, the Mondales are wonderful people. I liked the good-humored way he poked fun at himself, something I don't think I ever saw either Carter or Clinton do.

The election wasn't funny, however. Fourteen new Republican congressmen were swept in by the party's landslide victory. Half of them came from the South. It was a disaster, a death dance choreographed by the special interest groups.

Based purely on goodness, this well-intentioned man deserved better. But the campaign was doomed from the start. The groups just moved in and took him over lock, stock, and barrel. It wasn't hard; he sincerely believed in them and their ultra-liberal, out-of-the-mainstream philosophy. So from the get-go, NOW, AFL-CIO,

In the Oval Office with President Carter.

and NEA pumped the gas, punched the tickets, and steered the bus—and it was so obvious. Labor usually waited until after the convention to endorse, but not this time. They were like a kid at Christmas. They couldn't wait. Their grip was too tight. They were in the primaries and this, of course, just helped Gary Hart get support from the people outside the sway of the groups. Hart finished second in Iowa and surprised everyone by carrying New Hampshire. Mondale did defeat Hart in Georgia. It was in Atlanta that he asked Hart the question playing off the famous Wendy's commercial, "Where's the beef?"

The party nominated Geraldine Ferraro for vice president. But the historic nomination was tarnished because NOW chose to loudly boast they got it done. "Look at us, we did it." Truth is, they had. But it irritated voters when they so blatantly treated it as a quid pro quo. The convention in San Francisco would be long remembered. Jesse Jackson, who had been a candidate in 1984 and was already preparing to run again in 1988, would scream, "God is not through with me yet!" Then in a speech during prime time that went on forever, Mondale announced to the nation that one of the first things he would do was raise taxes. Hello? Goodbye. This 1984 election contrasted the differences between Democrats and Republicans more clearly than any election in recent times. When it was over, I looked at the wreckage and vowed never to get so involved again in a presidential campaign.

How Clinton Ran
and Won—Twice

Yes, I vowed to never again get so involved in national politics, and when 1988 rolled around, I didn't. Speaker Tom Murphy chose to help Al Gore, but ol' Brer Miller, he lay low. I did meet with Dick Gephardt as a favor to his colleague and my best friend, Congressman Ed Jenkins, but that was more a courtesy than involvement. The reelection campaign of Jimmy Carter and the abortive effort of Walter Mondale had soured me on National Democrats.

Of course, I couldn't resist watching the campaign intently from the sidelines. Atlanta hosted the Democratic National Convention and I studied the race as it developed. I couldn't get over how all the candidates handled fellow candidate Jesse Jackson with kid gloves no matter what he said. No matter how outrageous or extreme, no one would question or confront him. It was so servile it made them look more wimpy than tolerant. To the surprise of some, Jackson carried Georgia in the primary. I think part of the reason is Georgians flinched like I did as Michael Dukakis bragged about being a card-carrying member of the ACLU. In the South and many places elsewhere, that meant he was the guy who helped take down the nativity scene in front of city hall at Christmas.

After Dukakis got the nomination, I did break down and go to one rally. I went because someone in the campaign had the courage or naiveté to hold it in rural Georgia. It's next to impossible to get a national Democratic candidate to go anywhere in the state except to a labor or African-American event or fund-raiser in Atlanta. So, I went and was mortified when I saw the hay bales scattered around. Talk about hokey; it looked like the set from the "Hee Haw" television program. All Dukakis needed was a straw in his mouth. The only photo op that was worse was the one having him ride around in a tank like a tank commander. Instead of appearing macho as they had hoped, he barely peeped up out of it and looked silly and out of place. One pundit wrote, "like Mighty Mouse with a helmet on."

On the Republican side, Lee Atwater, a Southern-fried, guitar-plunking, good ole boy from South Carolina, was running the George H. W. Bush campaign. Atwater's brilliance was probably superfluous. The Democrats were self-destructing with another clueless campaign, resulting in another drubbing, especially in the South.

Ten states went Democratic (as well as the District of Columbia, which seldom votes for the president who gets to live there.) Forty states went for George Bush, the man they had jeered in Atlanta at the Democratic convention, characterizing him as "born with a silver foot in his mouth." That was a great red meat line, but it did little good as the Republicans won for the fifth time in six races and again carried every Southern state. In fact, of the 133 congressional districts in the South, the Democrats only carried twenty and they were the predominately African-American ones.

As the 1992 election loomed on the horizon, all eyes were on "the Hamlet of the Hudson," New York governor Mario Cuomo. He had toyed with the idea of running for years and without question

With President Clinton in the presidential limousine.

was a formidable presence. As a young man, he played minor league baseball in Georgia with the Brunswick Pirates and we once talked about those days. He remembered each little Georgia town, down to the details of the rickety wooden stands in those old Class D stadiums of the 1950s. I could imagine how powerful a television visual it would make for him to visit them again. South Georgians would accept him as one of their own, that is, until he proclaimed his position in opposition to capital punishment. But for some reason, Cuomo, the man with all the tools, could never bring himself to jump in. He was like that guy at the local swimming pool who would get up on the diving board and spring up and down, the very picture of a macho athlete, and then when all eyes were on him, he'd crawl down and go lay on his towel and work on his tan.

Bill Clinton had come within inches of running in 1988. He had consultants in place and had thought through the strategy. Then overnight he changed his mind. Those who were close to Clinton at this time, like consultants Raymond Strother and Dick Morris, believe it was Mrs. Clinton who said no. I had first met Bill and Hillary Clinton in 1982 when they came for dinner at the Georgia Governor's Mansion when Premier Deng Xiaoping of China was visiting Atlanta. Like nearly everyone who first met him, I was dazzled by Clinton. I never had any doubt that someday he would run for president. However, most of the polls believed that Carter had done so badly as president, he had ruined the chances for another Southerner for a long time. Of course, the experts underestimated how the peanut farmer from Plains could quickly rehabilitate his image in much the same dogged way he had run his races for governor and president. He became the best former president in history, erasing much of the stigma, and won the Nobel Peace Prize in 2003. They also underestimated the talents of Bill Clinton and they had no idea what a weak Democratic field there would be in 1992. The other choices were Jerry Brown, Tom Harkin, Bob Kerrey, and Paul Tsongas.

I was so enthralled by Arkansas's golden boy that in 1980 when I unsuccessfully ran for the Senate against incumbent Herman Talmadge, I hired Clinton's pollster and advisor, the very savvy Dick Morris. Twelve years later, with my strong recommendation, Clinton hired the brilliant team of James Carville and Paul Begala, who had worked for me when I ran for governor.

As governor of Arkansas, Clinton spent several nights at the Georgia Governor's Mansion. We came to know each other well. I remember once when he had spoken at our Richard Russell dinner, he wanted to stay afterwards to schmooze with the crowd as only he could do. I went on back home, leaving a state trooper to bring him later. A couple of hours later he came in. I asked if he was hungry. He said no, and we sat up a few more hours discussing politics before I finally excused myself and went to bed. One always had to do that with him because he would talk politics all night. The next morning, the state trooper who had brought him home the night before inquired, "Governor, is that man going to run for president?"

I said that I thought so. He replied, "Well, I'm going to vote for him, I'll tell you that. Last night he had me go by the drive-through window at McDonalds and he got two Big Macs and ate them both before we got back here [a distance that took less than five minutes]. Anyone who can eat like that I'm going to vote for."

As much as I liked Clinton and admired his great gifts, there was one thing that I found maddening about him. It was his habitual tardiness. He was never on time. Never!

Now, I'm at the extreme the other way. I'm obsessed with punctuality and I usually am always on time. I believe that keeping someone waiting is rude and says to them, "My time is more important than your time. I am more important than you." You cannot show respect for others if you do not respect the time of others. I believe chronic tardiness is symptomatic of even more serious flaws.

I had learned a great political lesson in the 1984 campaign with Walter Mondale beyond the realization that "the Groups," when given a grip, will always pull you under for their causes. That campaign I had a front-row seat for what Chris Matthews has called "the biggest con job in Democratic political history." It went like this: Bob Beckel, the able operative for Mondale, understood well the implications of the momentum Gary Hart had got from upsetting heavy favorite Mondale in New Hampshire. He knew the unexpected triumph put Hart on a roll with nine states holding upcoming primaries on what was called Super Tuesday.

But Beckel sensed that Mondale was in better shape in Georgia. With great hype and spin, Beckel deflected the Hart momentum by convincing the press corps ". . . this thing is going to come down to what happens in Georgia. Georgia is the key." The press swallowed it hook, line and sinker. All eyes were on Georgia, expecting to see Carter's old Veep bite the dust for good.

Well, of course, Mondale won Georgia. Then, Beckel announced it with great fanfare in a crowded Washington ballroom and all the networks made a huge deal out of it. Never mind that Hart carried seven of the nine states that day. Mondale had that "surprising" victory in Georgia. That was the big news.

I remembered the odd impact it had on the Mondale-Hart contest. I wondered if something like it could be made to happen again. There was no Super Tuesday as in 1984, but if Georgia could be the first Southern state to hold a primary after New Hampshire and if we could gin up the interest again and if Clinton could win, I could just envision the hoopla. Well, there just happened to be a germane bill in a state senate committee chaired by one of my closest friends and it could be changed just a little to push Georgia's primary up to an early date close on the heels of New Hampshire. I dispatched our state chairman, Ed Sims, another good friend and smooth operator, to get the Speaker and the attorney general and the national party's approval. It all fell into place and soon after "the Comeback Kid" had finished second in New Hampshire, he headed south and again all eyes were on Georgia.

Clinton did not disappoint and neither did Georgia. The first time he came to Georgia after New Hampshire we lined up so many supporters to appear on a platform with him that the sheer weight caused it to collapse. The word had gone forth, "If you ain't on that stage, you are out," and they were on the stage. From the inner city and the branch heads below the gnat line, they came and they liked what they saw. Clinton won Georgia by 57 percent. It was a blowout. Later, James Carville was to say, "Zell Miller was to Bill Clinton what John Sununu was to George Bush in 1988."

The young saxophone player hit all the right notes in a beautifully run campaign. At least the notes sounded sweet to my old rural middle-of-the-road ears: Tough on crime. Change welfare as we know it. The importance of merit and responsibility. A tax cut for the middle class. He always reminded voters he knew how to balance a budget, that he had done it time and time again in Arkansas.

"The economy, stupid" was a great slogan in that campaign and people bought into it. Just as important, though, was where Clinton the candidate stood on social issues. It came straight out of the play-book of the Democratic Leadership Council. I remember how he projected that stance at an event held outside the county welfare office in Jonesboro, Georgia, a blue-collar area a little south of Atlanta. It was one of those events that emphasized the "hit" of the day, "changing welfare as we know it." This was new and different rhetoric coming from a Democratic presidential candidate and it was exciting. He talked about "no more something for nothing" and changing that ingrained system. He said, "Welfare should be a second chance, not a way of life." He also talked—at this time—of punishing criminals, "not explaining away their behavior." This is what I had waited all my political life to hear from a national Democrat. My support for this man knew no bounds. And I was not alone. Little did we know what lay ahead.

Gennifer Flowers was a lounge singer and a former Arkansas state employee who claimed that she had had a long-time affair with Governor Clinton. The day the Gennifer Flowers feeding frenzy came to a head, Mrs. Clinton was spending the night with us at the Governor's Mansion in Atlanta. She and I were scheduled to fly around the next day, hitting some of the medium-sized cities many candidates will not take the time to do. All that night, lighted buttons on the phone beside my bed went on and off as calls came and went to the room in which she was staying. I could only imagine the turmoil that was going on and the words being said. I remembered another Democratic governor a few days before warning me that I was getting too far out front with Clinton and that "a high heel is about to fall."

The next morning, after a six-o'clock piece of toast for breakfast, Mrs. Clinton was ready to go. The first stop was Columbus, and after my introduction and endorsement she spoke for a few minutes and then took questions. No one was surprised by the first question, nor by the second and all the others on the same subject. If I've ever seen anyone, male or female, stand tall under pressure, I saw it that day. I continue to have great respect for this strong woman and even though over the years I've come to disagree with her on many, many issues, I cannot forget that day being in a fox hole with her and seeing up close the first evidence of Hillary the Warrior.

The Warrior gave me pause to think a few days later though, when she and her candidate-husband appeared on *60 Minutes*, and she made what I thought was a very unfair putdown of Tammy Wynette. Tammy was a friend and I can tell you, she was a woman who broke down barriers and was as gritty as they come. She was not the "stay at home and bake cookies" type at all, and her huge hit, "Stand By Your Man," was about the rock-solid value of commitment—a trait, ironically enough, that the first lady was to display herself a few years later.

Candidate Clinton survived, just as President Clinton would survive. It was uncanny. He continued even with all the distractions to talk about values and responsibility and commitment. Over and over he reminded us, "Governments don't raise children, people do." He took on Sister Soulja, the African-American rap singer, for her senseless remarks about blacks killing whites rather than blacks. He had the audacity—or political acumen—to do it with Jesse Jackson standing right there. He told the Rainbow Coalition her remarks were filled with hatred and "if you took the words 'white' and 'black' and reversed them, you might think David Duke was giving that speech." I thought back to 1988 when no candidate would have dared do that, just as today, none will challenge Al Sharpton on anything.

Clinton even asked the person with the thickest, twangiest Southern accent he could find to share the keynote evening at Madison Square Garden with the godlike voice of Barbara Jordan and the cerebral tone of Senator Bill Bradley. He called me at home in Young Harris and said he wanted me to tell the story of my mother, a single parent who had raised me and my sister during the Great Depression in that small mountain village. He had heard me tell it before and he said, "I want America to hear it."

They did.

Keynoting the Democratic National Convention in 1992.

My father—a teacher—died when I was two weeks old, leaving a young widow with two small children. But with my mother's faith in God—and Mr. Roosevelt's voice on the radio—we kept going. After my father's death, my mother, with her hands, cleared a small piece of rugged land. Every day she waded into a neighbors' cold mountain creek, carrying out hundreds of smooth stones to build a house. I grew up watching my mother complete that house from the rocks she'd lifted from the creek and cement she mixed in a wheelbarrow, cement that still today bears her hand-prints. Her son bears her handprints, too. She pressed her pride and dreams deep into my soul.

Clinton didn't know it, but I had long been a student of keynote speakers. In 1956, Governor Frank Clement of Tennessee—who at that time was known as the Boy Wonder—was speaking at the convention that nominated Adlai Stevenson. I had just gotten out of the Marines and was living in Athens. We had one baby, Murphy, and Matt was on the way. We had this grainy black-and-white TV and I was going to watch Clement's speech that night. About four o'clock that afternoon, Shirley went into labor. I took her to St. Mary's hospital. At five, six, and seven o'clock, she was still in labor. When the baby hadn't come by then, I began to wonder if I was going to miss that keynote speech, so I went home and watched. I can still remember parts of it. Clement talked about President Eisenhower "gazing down the fairways of indifference." It was a great speech. When I got back to the hospital, Matthew had already arrived. A few years ago I met Frank Clement's son, Bob, who was then in Congress. I told him I would never forget August 13, 1956, the night his father spoke. He took a step back and asked how I could remember the exact date. I laughed and told him that was the night my second son was born.

In the general election, Ross Perot almost screwed up the works. After getting in and getting out and getting in again, he ended up with nearly 20 million votes or 19 percent. Clinton got 43 percent and Bush 37 percent. Clinton carried four Southern states, Arkansas, Georgia, Louisiana, and Tennessee, as well as the border states of Kentucky and Missouri.

Most would agree that the campaign did not portend what was to come. The transition was run as badly as the campaign had been well run. Political correctness ran amok within a general atmosphere of chaos. To get a cabinet that "looked like America" became the overriding consideration, much more important than merit. Overnight the "new Democrat" had become the "old liberal." The "third way" had become the "old way." Clinton's position of "Don't ask, don't tell" for gays in the military made both gays and the military mad. That was followed with advocacy for gun control and a ten-day waiting period not far behind. His (mostly Hillary's) health care initiative was so far out even the Democratic Congress wouldn't consider it. When he later raised taxes, it sent Buddy Darden and Don Johnson, two good middle-of-the-road Georgia Democratic congressmen who voted for it, back home. No wonder that at midterm in 1994 when the voters got to speak again they screamed; it was one of the biggest earthquakes to hit Washington in many years. For the first time in forty years Republicans captured Congress and it was no squeaker. They gained fifty-two votes in the House and eight in the Senate. It was an historic achievement, orchestrated almost single-handedly by Newt Gingrich of Georgia with help, of course, from the President.

Oh, sure, the Comeback Kid with all his skills and luck would come back. But his party wouldn't . . . and hasn't. How did he do it? Over the years, I've watched many experienced politicians get into trouble, including yours truly. Invariably when that happens we all react the same. We turn to the familiar and what worked for us before. In Clinton's case, enter Dick Morris again, as he had before when Clinton was trying to come back from a humiliating defeat after a two-year term as governor of Arkansas. Morris has called the strategy "triangulation," which to me means taking some of the best issues of your opposition and using them as your own with a

Stumping through Georgia with Bill Clinton and Al Gore in 1992.

slightly different spin. Make it a positive spin instead of a negative spin. Be "for," not "against." Be "pro," not "anti." George Stephanopoulos, who often resented Morris' influence over the president, put it this way: "Capture the center ideologically, politically, morally, and culturally." It was a strategy aimed directly at that 25 percent of the electorate known as the "value voters."

There were many bits and pieces that led to Clinton's reelection, but basically over nearly a two-year period it came down to three main thrusts. One: the balanced budget speech to the nation by the president in June 1995. It led to the fight that ultimately climaxed with the closing down of the government for several days in November that year. There had been a long, drawn-out fight between Clinton and the Republican Congress over the budget. When the fiscal year ended in October without a budget in place, government came to a standstill and the Congressional Republicans got the blame, not the President. Two: a massive negative ad

campaign that demonized Speaker Newt Gingrich along with
Senator Bob Dole and the rest of the Republican Congress thrown
in. It cost tens of millions of dollars, mostly soft money, and inexpli-
cably went completely unanswered by the Republicans until it was
too late. Newt has estimated 125,000 of these very effective ads ran.
Three: the most brilliant, as well as the longest, State of the Union
speech in 1996. The president hit all the right notes on all the right
issues from anti-crime to welfare with fiscal responsibility thrown in
for good measure. It was aimed directly at Middle America and
those value voters. Shirley and I were in the gallery and my hands
grew sore from clapping. It was a political masterpiece. Clinton's
numbers a few days later were 53-36, and they stayed there most of
the election year.

Unfortunately, it was just so much campaign strategy, a chess
game played with the pawns on the board by a master. It had no
core belief except winning. I do not condemn, for I have done much
the same—just not as well. No one in politics wants to lose, and we
rationalize that the end will justify the means. Could Lincoln have
freed the slaves if not first having played some of the crassest politics possible in order to get the nomination and then win?

I care not to get into what happened that second term with
Monica and the lies and the meaning of "is" and the impeachment
and the pardons and yes, the great economy. I prefer to remember
those two campaigns with their almost perfectly pitched mantra of
values that somehow, except for welfare reform, just sort of evapo-
rated into the thin air of Washington. But for a few brief moments,
before all the stuff hit the fan, the Democratic Party had a candidate
I could identify with and was willing to fight for. What was it the
poet said? "For of all sad words of tongue or pen, the saddest are
these: It might have been."

DAYS OF WHINE AND ROSE-COLORED GLASSES

24

The trouble with too many Democrats today is that they had rather make a statement than win an election. They just want to make their point . . . loudly!

That is not true, however, about the Democratic Leadership Council. The week after the election in November 2004, there's going to be a lot of empty-feeling Democrats in their sackcloth and ashes wishing they had listened to Al From, Bruce Reed, and pollster Mark Penn, who warned in July 2003, "The Democratic Party is hurt by current perceptions that Democrats stand for big government, want to raise taxes too high, are too liberal, and are beholden to special interest groups. Half a century ago a near majority of voters identified themselves a part of the Democratic Party. Today that number has declined to roughly one-third." Frankly, in my opinion, it's more than "perception"; it's reality.

But as always, most of the national Democratic crowd had rather listen to the politically tone-deaf special interest brokers who are totally ignorant of the real-world political landscape. Bill

Clinton was the exception. But he would always wait until the boat was taking water and listing. Then, right before an election, he would start bailing.

One of the popular declarations of the special interests this political season is "We don't need a Republican-lite." As usual, they miss the point entirely; it's not about being "Republican-lite" or "Bush Lite"; it's about being where most of the voters are, especially as it relates to those all-important electoral votes. They are always completely fooled by large, enthusiastic crowds, conveniently forgetting, for example, that Walter Mondale was drawing huge numbers in New York City and Chicago just a few days before losing forty-nine states.

It also has to do with "the sensible center," not the loony left, which is the habitat of the Democrat's special interest groups. You ask, don't the Republicans have their special interests groups also? You bet they do. But the difference is the grand pooh-bahs of the Democratic groups insist on front row seats and demand that a lot of fuss be made over them. They are very high maintenance and they want everyone to know they are the tail that wags this dog. The Republican special interest groups, to the contrary, are content to operate under the radar. They've learned to conduct their politics without all the fanfare. They've lowered their voices and moved around as stealthily as deacons at the VFW bar. With them, it's about winning, not ego or who gets the credit. On the other hand, with the special interest Demos, they might as well be dressed in band uniforms like the Music Man, strutting down the street with trombones blaring and clarinets screeching, "Hey Look Me Over, Lend Me Your Ear".

It has to do with being a mature national party, not a hodge-podge of special interest groups, which undeniably is what the national Democratic Party has become. Look at California, where the "extremes" held that state in their grip until it went belly-up. Just a preview of coming attractions, I'm afraid.

No Democrat wants to tell the leaders of their party that they have halitosis. But they do and it cannot be improved with a little mouthwash right before that date they have every other year with the South. In 2002, the Democrats lost the governorships in Georgia, South Carolina, and Alabama. Truth to tell, this cannot be blamed entirely on the national Democratic Party. Those three good Democratic governors, Roy Barnes, Jim Hodges, and Don Siegelman, will tell you they share some of the blame themselves. But the axis of McAuliffe, Clinton, Gore, and Daschle, dominated by the "Groups," created an atmosphere so bad that it is almost impossible for Democrats to be heard in that "one-third of a nation." With a "D" after their names, candidates in the South today start out with two strikes against them.

Since their defeats in 2002, it has only gotten worse, negating years of hard work on their part and many who came before them who wanted to stay loyal to their party heritage but were left needing oxygen. Trying to win the U.S. Senate seats we now hold in Georgia, Florida, South Carolina, and North Carolina is going to be a hard row to hoe. The reason: the poor reputation and the record of the national Democratic Party.

All of this has escaped the party leaders until now that it's too late. They always have their own take on what the problem is and talking with them is like talking to a fence post. Believe me, I've tried. They sincerely believe those Washington-based strategists understand the problem better than those who live in the South and have run successful campaigns there for years.

As much as I deplore my party's reputation for sucking up to these left-leaning special interest groups, there is another rip in our heritage, in our image, that I regret even more. I fear some of the Democratic presidential candidates are treading on very dangerous ground for the party, and, more importantly, for the country. I do not question their patriotism; I question their judgment. They are doing what politicians often do, playing to the loudest, most active, and most emotional group of supporters, feeding off their frustration while clawing to find some advantage. I've done it myself and lived to regret it.

My concern is that, without meaning to, they are exacerbating the difficulties of a nation at war. A demagogue is defined by Webster as "a political leader who gains power by arousing people's emotions and prejudices." Isn't that exactly what some of them are doing? Some of the liberal media excuse these actions by calling them "populism." Populism, my butt! Its demagogy, pure and simple. They should stop this, or at least modify it into a more civil discourse.

Howard Dean, while not alone, is the worst offender, and it says a lot about the current Democratic base that he has emerged as the frontrunner for the Democratic nomination for president. He likes to say he belongs to the Democratic wing of the Democratic Party, but I say he belongs to the whining wing of the Democratic Party. Angry and red-faced, these doom-and-gloomers need to take some "calm-me-down" pills. Over the years I've learned to beware of candidates who yell and scream and jump up and down. Usually what they're saying has so little substance they have to make up for it with histrionics. But they should realize that their overheated rhetoric is dividing the country when they should be helping unite it.

Republican presidential candidate Wendell Wilkie didn't stoop to this demagogy in 1940 when he ran against President Roosevelt during those dangerous times on the eve of World War II. And Neville Chamberlain didn't do it to Winston Churchill, who had replaced him as prime minister. They understood there are some things more important than making political points when a nation is in peril.

Frankly, I cannot understand their shrill, manufactured opposition. Think about it. We've freed a nation from a cruel and oppressive dictator. A free Iraq, most everyone agrees, can transform the Middle East. Isn't that what presidents have wanted to do for many years? Give it time. Of course it's going to be difficult. Of course it's going to be costly. Regrettably, more of our American sons and daughters will die. There will be times when it looks like it's not worth it. But in the long stretch of history, it will be worth it.

Senator John McCain and other well-informed leaders have called Iraq "the central battle on the war on terror." I believe that. Condoleezza Rice spoke plainly and truthfully when she called it a "generational commitment." For someone like me with grandchildren and great-grandchildren, whom I love more than life itself, that is a hard and sobering thought.

But with all I've learned from study, age, and experience, I believe, with every fiber of my body, that there comes a time when a civilization has to choose between good and evil, between freedom and tyranny. One of the greatest lessons history has taught us over and over again is that the choice we make between good and evil will reverberate for generations to come. It could make the world a safer place for my grandchildren and great-grandchildren. It is worth the risk.

It gives me great comfort and security to know that President Bush and his advisors understand this and will not be deterred. Of course, the future is dangerous. That is the job description of the future: to be dangerous. But we learn from history that humanity's greatest achievements have occurred during the periods of greatest danger.

I like the fact that the Bush White House is not timid about making a decision and does not suffer from "analysis paralysis," the malady that is common to those learned people "who know so much and can see all sides." Unfortunately, these mostly well-intentioned persons see so many shades of gray, they often miss the black and white. And that is what is called for today.

So, now I have had my say. It's a habit of mine. I recall that trait from as far back as nearly sixty years ago when I was a barefoot lad growing up in Young Harris and wading in mud holes. Down the road from our house lived the area's most successful mule trader. Each Monday he would load five or six mules in the back of his truck and go over the mountain to the sale barn. There he'd sell or trade them for different mules. He was good at it and supported a large family with his shrewdness.

For the uninformed, mules have a mind of their own. In the South, the terms "stubborn as a mule" or "mule-headed" are used to describe highly independent people. One has to deal with a mule on its own terms, kind of like cats. Mules are very different from horses. You can ride or work a horse until it just falls dead or can go no more. Not so with mules; they will balk when they get tired and refuse to budge.

My neighbor never kept any mule very long. Sometimes he'd trade all six and come back late in the afternoon with a new half dozen. He considered it bad luck not to make at least a single trade. One summer day he brought back the most beautiful mule any of us had ever seen. Sleek, with rippling muscles, alert eyes, and long ears that were almost like velvet. For weeks he kept her. Week in and week out, he'd take her just to show her off and then bring her back.

One morning I was out in the yard and could see that he was doing some work around the barn. Curious, I went down to inspect. He had a car jack and had jacked up one corner of the barn and put several flat rocks in the old foundation to raise that side of the structure about six inches.

I followed him as he moved to the next corner where he already had the flat rocks ready. For the first time he spoke to his young onlooker, "I'm going to raise the ceiling; those old, low-hanging rafters are tearing up my mule's ears." I had noticed the once-beautiful ears were looking a little ragged and ratty but didn't know why.

Wise beyond my years, or so I thought, I decided to give my neighbor the benefit of my young and agile mind, "Why don't you just dig out the floor of the stable?" (It was a dirt floor.) He stopped with a jerk and glared at the young know-it-all, who was daring to tell him how to do the job. Obviously aggravated, he said, "Son, you don't understand the problem. It's not the mule's legs that are too long, it's her ears."

"Son, you don't understand the problem." I have frequently thought about those words when I have been tempted to tell someone how to run their business. So, as my writing on this "how to" book winds down, that boyhood experience of blurting out my advice is recalled again. But, in this case, I know a lot more about politics than I did mules.

* * * * * * * * *

Nearly fifty years ago, soon after Shirley and I were married and living in that little trailer at Camp Lejune, N.C., we got into our first minor domestic spat. She did not take kindly to my advice on how to improve her chicken potpie. Before we had time to properly make up, I was assigned to the rifle range as a coach and had to stay with the troops in the barracks at Camp Geiger.

Firing on the range started at daybreak and was over around noon. As the men cleaned their weapons, the coaches had a few hours to kill. With our disagreement fresh in my mind, with no phone and the regret that I'd said anything about the quality of her cooking, I composed a little poem I called "Words of Advice on the Subject of Advice." I sent it to the *Raleigh News and Observer*, which printed poems in the lower left-hand corner of their editorial page. I used the name Drew Rellim (Miller spelled backwards) for I did not want my fellow "Jarheads" to know they had a budding poet in their midst. It was printed the following week.

I hadn't thought of this in years but after more than two hundred pages of "advice" on subjects much deeper than a chicken potpie, I remembered this incident and recalled the poem's last two lines, "Would you save your heart from aches, let her make her own mistakes."

Perhaps I should have remembered my mule trader neighbor's "no help wanted" sign and those lines of advice to myself about letting someone "make their own mistakes." But, with this book, I just couldn't help taking one more whack at trying to talk a little sense into the party I've been part of since birth. I suppose, in the winter of my life, I could have just smiled, kept my mouth shut, attended the parties, and enjoyed the trips. I could have gone along and gotten along and become just another piece of furniture in that exclusive club. I could have served my time and then quietly gone back to those Southern hills I came from. But, when I saw what I saw and heard what I heard, that conscience I wrote about in the first chapter just wouldn't let me.

INDEX